William Griffiths

A Practical Treatise on Farriery

Deduced from the experience of above fifty years in the services of the grandfather and father of Sir Watkin Williams Wynn, Bart., the present Earl Grosvenor, and the present Sir Watkin Williams Wynn, Bart.

William Griffiths

A Practical Treatise on Farriery
Deduced from the experience of above fifty years in the services of the grandfather and father of Sir Watkin Williams Wynn, Bart., the present Earl Grosvenor, and the present Sir Watkin Williams Wynn, Bart.

ISBN/EAN: 9783337221454

Printed in Europe, USA, Canada, Australia, Japan

Cover: Foto ©Lupo / pixelio.de

More available books at **www.hansebooks.com**

H. Bunbury Esq. Delin.   W. Dickinson Excudit

London, Publish'd Oct. 21, 1784 by W. Dickinson.

A

PRACTICAL TREATISE,

ON

FARRIERY;

DEDUCED FROM THE

EXPERIENCE OF ABOVE FIFTY YEARS,

IN THE

SERVICES,

OF

The Grandfather and Father, of Sir Watkin Williams Wynn, Bart.

The present Earl Grosvenor,

AND,

The present Sir Watkin Williams Wynn, Bart.

THE SECOND EDITION, WITH ADDITIONS.

By WILLIAM GRIFFITHS, late Groom, at Wynnstay.

> Kind Sir, if you should lame your Tit,
> Peruse what's in these Pages writ;
> The Blockhead Smith, you first may see
> Will swear he's lame ABOVE the Knee,
> When, (as this Treatise plain will shew,)
> 'Tis ten to one, he's lame BELOW.

PRINTED BY J. MARSH.

AT THE DRUID PRESS,

1795.

ENTERED AT STATIONERS HALL.

To the Right Hon. Earl Grosvenor,

And, to Sir Watkin Williams Wynn, Bart.

My Lord and Hon. Sir,

The great Obligations I have been under to two such worthy Personages, as Earl Grosvenor my late Master, and Sir Watkin Williams Wynn, Bart. my present Master; makes me not hesitate a Moment, to whose Protection I should commit the following Sheets, and it is with the greatest Pleasure and Satisfaction that I have an Opportunity of publishing them under your Protection and Approbation.

Farriery is a Science I early in Life coveted the Knowledge of, and in the Stables and Service of the late worthy Sir Watkin Williams Wynn, Bart. at Wynnstay, I first began my Practice, as then Under-groom to Mr. Richard Sidebotham, and which I have since pursued with the greatest Attention through every Stage of Life; I must beg Leave to acknowledge during the Time I had the Honor to serve your Lordship, I had great Opportunities of Improvement by the Numbers of Horses young and old, that fell under

DEDICATION.

my Confideration, many of the Cafes were defperate, both internal and external; I muft likewife beg Leave to acknowledge the greateft Sincerity my late Mafter Sir Watkin Williams Wynn, Bart. fhewed me, refpecting my Return to Wynnftay again, in the Year, 1772, where I have purfued the above Science to the utmoft of my Power, and at my leifure Hours have put together the following Sheets, as they are the Work of my own Labor, and by the Advice of my Friends, I give them the Public in my own Language, fubmitting to their Candor my want of Education neceffary for a Writer.

I muft acknowledge my great Obligation to Henry Bunbury, Efq. for the Frontifpiece to this Work, which is a great Ornament; likewife, I am under Obligations to the Gentlemen Subfcribers, with my fincere Wifhes that it may prove wholly agreeable to their Expectations; and, with every due Refpect, for the many Favors received from Earl Grofvenor, and Sir Watkin Williams Wynn, Bart.

I fubfcribe myfelf,

    My Lord and Hon. Sir,

        Your moft dutiful and obliged Servant,

            William Griffiths.

Wynnftay, Aug. 8th. 1795.

Wm. Griffiths.

THE

PREFACE.

****

My Honorable Friends and Worthy Gentlemen;

As I have attempted a Thing of this Kind, I mean it should be as plain and as perfect as possible to be understood, and not to darken you with false Explanations; but mean to give the best and readiest undoubted Methods of my own *Practice*, to obtain the Cure of every Disorder in each *Section*, in a very plain and easy Manner; as so, I do advise the Practitioner of the following Work to be duly careful in reading every *Section* over separately and give true Attention to the whole *Section*; especially the *Section* that relates to the Disorder or Calamity that he means to treat or handle at that present Time; by so doing, all the whole Work will become easy and quite familiar to the Practitioner. And further, I say, to be duly cautious in reading the Symptoms in the beginning of each *Section*, and to be certain of the particular Symptoms, and in so doing will enable him to be truly satisfied with the Disorder, and not mistake the Symptoms; as there are several Symptoms similar

to

PREFACE.

to each other in several of the Cases. Further, I say, of the ill Effects of bad dead Drugs, as are at sometimes substituted instead of good; the above ill Method has caused the Death of several Horses; therefore, I will advise all men that make use of Drugs, to procure them from the best Markets, and not to trust to bad of any kind. Good and well prepared Drugs are noble Articles, and very bad are entirely dangerous; and in my Opinion, the fittest Place to receive them is the Mixen or Dunghill.

Let this be a Precaution to all Men that administer Medicines to Horses, to be duly cautious in giving Medicines of any kind, before they point out the true Disorder, and not to cram the poor Creatures with this, that, and the other kind of Medicines, but give proper Time for every sort of Medicine or Dose to act or operate; before you administer or repeat the second or third Dose, &c. By so doing, you will give Nature fair play, and enable the Animal to withstand the Shocks of such robust Medicines, as are very proper to be given in some Cases; but on the other hand, proper Time enables the Medicine to take its due Course, and act according to your Expectations.

Further, I say, in regard to outward Applications and Operations. First of the Errors of probing, cutting and provoking of a Wound when dressed. The above *Practice* commonly brings on a Mortification.

PREFACE.

If a Wound or Ulcer requires cutting, cut it once properly the whole Length of the Cavity; but do not open the Wound too soon after the firſt Dreſſing, but rather omit a day or two longer to give the Wound time to come to a good Digeſtion, before you open it; then act according to the following Directions, and give every Application time to work its due Efficacy, according as they are compounded, and always give Nature fair play; then there is no doubt of Succeſs and doing well, if the Practitioner will give himſelf time to forethink, and judge properly of Precautions relating to the following Work.

I do not expect this Work to eſcape Cenſure; neither have I the Ambition to think it free from Imperfection. Yet upon the whole I think, I have given true Directions, which are entirely from my own *Practice*. If ſome ſhould differ from me in Opinion, I ſhall not be angry; and I hope, it will in ſome meaſure defend me from Cenſure, that I am willing to give others the ſame Liberty, as I deſire to have myſelf, that is, a Liberty to follow their own Judgments.

W. G.

A TABLE OF WEIGHTS, COMMONLY USED IN PHYSIC.

20 Grains,	1 Scruple,
3 Scruples,	1 Dram,
8 Drams,	1 Ounce,
12 Ounces,	1 Pound.

ERRATA.

Page 12, Line 23, for Buckthrön, read Buckthorn.
—— 32, —— 15, for ond read and.
—— 39, —— 8, for pape, read page.
—— 41, —— 17, for odd, read add.
—— 53, —— 30, for 81, read 82.
—— 55, —— 2, for 81, read 82.
—— 94, —— 17, for point, read pint.
—— 168, —— 24, for Ticture, read Tincture.

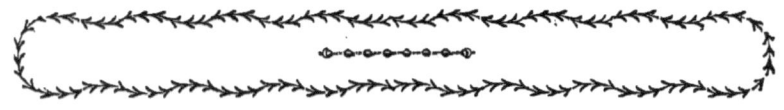

A

PRACTICAL TREATISE,

ON

FARRIERY.

Section 1.

Of the PULSE *of a* HORSE.

THE regular Pulse of a Horse in health, beats forty times in one minute; if much less, it denotes lowness, if fifty, or more, it denotes a high fever, therefore, according to the number, to be termed higher or lower, and so judge accordingly, as symptoms should appear. The Pulse is to be felt between the point of the shoulder and the setting on of the neck, above the breast, on the lower part of the neck vein.— The Pulse is difficult to be felt in the above part, but shall mention a readier part to feel it, as follows. Set your hand on the side of the chest, opposite the heart, about a span behind the elbow; there you will feel the heart Pulse beat plainly.

Of FEVERS *in General.*

Horses are subject to Fevers from accidents, from severe wounds, from catching a severe cold or by overheating by severe work in hot weather, and bad management after it.—

one of the above doses three times a-day, mixed with a pint of Red Port Negus, made weak. The above to be repeated until such time you see his body fortified; and his cold and hot sweats quite abated.

To be given in the RECOVERY of a FEVER, to cause an APPETITE.

Take Jesuits Bark one ounce, Gentian half an ounce, Salt of Tartar half an ounce, Elixir of Vitriol one dram, to be given in a quart of warm Ale, every other day, or as occasion may be required.

To promote URINE in a FEVER.

Take Salt Prunella one ounce, Juniper Berries, and Venice Turpentine of each half an ounce, and Diapente one ounce, made up into a ball with Barbadoes Tar, for one dose. Give one of the above balls, every other morning; or according as they operate; or as symptoms may require the use of them.

To be given if COSTIVE in a FEVER.

Take Lenitive Electuary three ounces, Cream of Tartar two ounces, Sweet Oil six ounces, Glauber's Salts three ounces, and Treacle half a pound. Dissolve the above in a quart of Watergruel, for one dose; this will open his body mild and easy, and pass quick. To be repeated as symptoms may require the use of it, that is, in three or four days to come.

To be given in the RECOVERY of a FEVER.

Take Liver of Antimony one pound and a half, made into very fine powder, Nitre Salts half a pound, Flour of Brimstone half a pound. Mix the above all together, and keep it in a bladder for use. Give of the above alterative powders, a table-spoonful once or twice a-day, in a mash of scalded Bran

and

Of FEVERS.

and Oats. Alſo it would be proper to indulge a Horſe in the recovery of a Fever. To lead him out in hand for an hour, in the warmeſt part of the day, and there let him pick and nip ſome freſh Graſs, in a good paſture: or rather, if poſſible to be met with, ſome green blades of Rye. The above method will cool and refreſh him much, if repeated.

Proper FOOD to be given in FEVERS.

Make uſe of Watergruel to drink, when dry, as often as you can, and Bran, with very little Oats ſcalded together for maſhes, but if coſtive, give Rye inſtead of Oats with the Bran. Give a ſmall maſh of the above two or three times a-day, and let him nuzzle, and pick ſome ſweet Wheat Straw, and no other kind of food for ſome days together: at the ſame time give Nitre Salts, diſolved in all his water; or according as ſymptoms may require the uſe of it. But if his appetite is quite gone, he muſt be indulged with ſweet Milk, ſweetened with brown Sugar, three or four times a-day, and give him four, or five hornfuls at a time. But do not be alarmed if a Horſe is without meat in a Fever for a-day or two; ſo that he ſucks a little Watergruel, and nips a little clean Wheat Straw. Never cram nor force a Horſe to eat in the beginning of a Fever; for he ſeldom will take any hurt for the firſt two or three days for want of food; ſo as there are true precautions taken, in giving his medicines, as before directed. I have often ſeen Horſes full in fleſh, in a lingering Fever, not making the leaſt ſigns of a recovery, until they had loſt much fleſh, and had no appearance to be droughty or thirſty, during their whole illneſs.— Therefore I would adviſe the practitioner in the above caſe, to make uſe of the intermitting compound Fever Balls, ſee page 3d. as there directed, in all reſpects.

Section,

Section, 2.

Of STAGGERS *and* CONVULSIONS.

STAGGERS, is a common cafe to Horfes; efpecially in the latter end of the fummer. And moſt commonly affects heavy draught Horfes and fo-forth. The general caufe of the above diforder is, when grafs becomes dry and lacks a moiſture; and thereby locks and clogs the bowels and guts with fuch a great load of hard dry excrement; alfo brings on a great coſtivenefs; and generally flies into the head as a Vertigo; and caufes Convulfions and Fevers. The chief fymptoms of the above diforder, are, a Horfe will be ſtiff in his whole frame, appearing dull, and fwelled about his head and eyes; with his eyes ſtaring upwards, he will reel and ſtagger to and fro, like unto a drunken man; and by preſſing againſt his forehead, he will thruſt forward againſt your hand, and if the fymptom is very violent, he will puſh and thruſt his head up to the rack; and there will fpar and heave like a draught Horfe, as if he would thruſt through the rack; and generally has an appearance of the Yellows and Jaundice. In the firſt ſtage of the above cafe, bleed plentifully, that is, open three or four veins at one time, fo let him bleed four or five quarts, and at the fame time fet in the Animal two rowels, one in the forehead and the other in the briſket. Then immediately give as follows.

A Spirituous DRAUGHT *for the* STAGGERS.

Take Friar's Balfam and Spirits of Salvolatile of each one ounce, Spirits of Salt Ammoniac half an ounce; all mixed and
ſhook

Of STAGGERS.

shook in a bottle together, and given as a drink; the above has given immediate ease in this obstinate case; then immediately give the following Clyster.

A CLYSTER for the STAGGERS.

Take Sena two ounces, and boil it in two quarts of Water for half an hour; then strain the decoction off, and add Syrup of Buckthorn two ounces, common Treacle one pound, and Sweet Oil half a pint, dissolve the whole together: then given immediately. The above Clyster to be repeated three times a-day if occasion be. If the above Clyster should not sufficiently empty the great gut, make use of the strong Clyster for the Staggers. See page 12. Before you administer any Clyster; first rake him with a small hand and arm, then administer the Clyster. Then immediately give the following cooling purge, if required:

A Cooling PURGE for the STAGGERS,

Take Lenitive Electuary three ounces, Cream of Tartar two ounces, Glauber's Salts three ounces, Flour of Brimstone two ounces, common Treacle one pound and Sweet Oil half a pint: all dissolved in a pint of Ale for one dose. The above will cause him to purge mild and easy, and pass quick: or you may make use of the following Purge.

An Easy PURGE for the STAGGERS.

Take Cream of Tartar two ounces, Glauber's Salts three ounces, Flour of Brimstone three ounces, Nitre Salts two ounces, Jalap four drams, and common Treacle one pound, Sweet Oil half a pint. Dissolve the above in a pint of Ale for one dose. This will cause him to purge mild and easy and pass quick. The above Purges to be repeated as symptoms may require the use of them.

A Stimulating

Of STAGGERS.

A Stimulating EMBROCATION for the STAGGERS.

Take Muſtard Seed in fine Powder four ounces, Spirits of Wine half a Pint, Camphire one ounce, diſſolved in the above Spirits; then mix the above altogether in a bottle for uſe, then rub the Animal's Head all round with the above Mixture, his Pall and Glands, and obſerve to rub it well in, and repeat it often in the day, by ſo doing will revive him much, eſpecially if it ſhould be of the ſleepy kind; the above application will likewiſe releave a locked Jaw.

A BALL for the STAGGERS.

Take Myrrh half an ounce, Saffron and Caſtor, of each one dram, Cinnabar of Antimony half an ounce, Gum Galbanum two drams, Aſſafœtida four drams; and Emetic Tartar half a dram, made up into a ball with the Powers of Amber, for one doſe. The above to be given once a-day, or omit the ball as occaſion may require the diſuſe of it.

The MITHRIDATE I now uſe, or PASTE.

Take Anniſeeds four ounces, Turmeric, Elicampane, Liquorice Root, Gentian, Birthwort, Sena, Flour of Brimſtone, Cream of Tartar, Torment Rhubarb, Myrrh, Juniper Berries, Gum Arabic, Scordium, Ginger, Vervain Root, Valerian, of each two ounces, all in fine powder, Saffron chopped ſmall one ounce, Sweet Oil eight ounces; make the whole into a Paſte, with equal parts of Honey and Common Treacle, then keep it cloſe in a pot for uſe; the above is a good Medicine, to be given in the Staggers; the doſe of the above is two ounces, diſſolved in a quart of Ale, to which add half an ounce of my Anodyne Balſam; or might be given in any ſleepy, drowſy caſe alone, without the Anodyne Balſam added to it.

Proper

Of STAGGERS.

Proper Food to be given in the STAGGERS.

Let them be often fupplied with Watergruel well boiled, for their common drinking, and fupport them with Maſhes made of Wheat Bran and a little Rye fcalded together as food, alfo to indulge them two or three times a-day with a pint of Sweet Milk, fweetened with Brown Sugar; the above will affift nature for a long time, without any other fupport.

For a wild Fit of the STAGGERS.

Take Mithridate two ounces, diffolved in a quart of fmall Ale, then add Tincture of Saffron and Camphire one ounce and a half, fee page 37. Tincture of Opium two drams, the Powers of Amber two drams, and Common Treacle half a pound, mixed all together for one dofe. The above will compofe and lull him to fleep; by being covered up very warm—will bring on a ftrong fweat, then if poffible, to get him to a hot horfe-mixen or dunghill, make him a bed and caft him down there, and cover him with warm muck all over, except his mouth and noftrils; and encourage the fweating for four hours at leaft: then obferve to cool him gradually; and remember, in this, and all fuch cafes, to make ufe of Chewing Balls which are to be made as follows. Take Affafœtida one ounce, and Savin a fmall handful; bruife them together in a mortar into a ball; then tie the whole in a linen cloth to the middle part of a fnaffle-bit; then let the faid bit, be put into the Horfe's mouth and fo let him chew it for one hour, then take it off for an hour, and fo off and on every other hour, until his fymptoms abate.

Alfo, Aloes alone is a good Chewing Ball, in the above diforder, and to be made ufe of as the latter.

The said Ball is very serviceable for Horses in the Staggers; also, in the Falling Evil, and Convulsions.

The use of the above Balls is, to quicken the motion of the head and membrane, or the net that covers the brain. The above, being repeated, will free the head; and cause him to slobber and slaver, and the like evacuations. But if the above disorder should continue longer than common, and the Animal has taken to lie down much, make use of the following for the last remedy.

Take Quicksilver and pour two drams of it into each ear, and shake it well into the head. The above has done wonderful cures to the astonishment of many.

Section, 3.

Of YELLOWS or JAUNDICE.

THE cause of the Yellows, is, commonly from a stone in the gall-bladder, or decay of the liver. Although, I may justly say, that I never could find a gall-bladder in a Horse; but without doubt, there must be a gall-pipe in the liver, to assist the chyle or food to a digestion. The symptoms of the Yellows, are a great heaviness and weakness: a Horse will be very feeble in all his actions, and seem to breathe fainty, with deep sighs, and his appetite quite gone: the white of his eyes, his mouth and lips, and the roof of his mouth, will appear yellow, and also his urine yellow: he will seem very weak, and has the appearance of a slow Fever. I have known a Horse so weak in the Jaundice, that he could not walk a Mile: in the above disorder, make use of the following directions.

A Drink

Of JAUNDICES.

A Drink for the YELLOWS.

Take Sweet Milk a pint and a half, and make a poffet with ftrong Beer, ftrain it off, and add to the whey, Caftile Soap one ounce fliced thin, Salendine a handful chopped fmall, and boil them together; then add to the above, Saffron chopped fmall one dram; and give it as a drink, every other day, fafting. Repeat three or four drinks; give the Horfe warm Water, and very gentle exercife the interval days, that he has not his drink given him.

For the YELLOW JAUNDICE.

Take Rue, Wormwood, Hyffop, Salendine and Red Sage of each, a fmall handful, chopped and pounded together in a mortar--then add Turmeric two ounces, Caftile Soap two ounces, and Saffron one dram; beat the whole together in a mortar, and add as much frefh Butter as will form the whole into four balls. Give one of the above balls, every morning, fafting; or diffolved in a quart of mild Ale. Obferve to give warm Water, and Mafhes, during the time the drink is given.

For the YELLOWS.

Take the Mithridate I now ufe, take of the above Pafte two ounces, to which add one ounce and a half of Caftile Soap to the above Pafte. Give the whole for one drink, in a quart of Ale; give three of the above drinks, one every other day. Pafte, fee page 8.

A Powerful Ball for the YELLOWS when Obftinate.

Take Turmeric and Diapente of each two ounces, Tincture of Martis four drams, Caftile Soap and Cinnabar of Antimony of each two ounces, and Saffron two drams; made up with Honey, and divided into four balls. Give one of the above balls every morning fasting; or as symptoms may require the use of them.

Also a Ball for the JAUNDICE.

Take Bracken's Cordial Ball one pound, see page 28.— Æthiops Mineral three ounces, Castile Soap four ounces, small red Earth Worms, well cleaned in Moss two ounces, and Saffron two drams, made up with Honey, into balls.— Give one ball weighing two ounces, for one dose. Give one of the above balls every morning fasting. At the same time, it would be proper to give warm Water and Mashes, during the time of his disorder; indulging him with gentle exercise, every afternoon during the time he takes his medicines; which will greatly add to the cure of the Jaundice. In the recovery of the above disorder, it will be proper to give an easy gentle Purge or two; I would recommend the Hiera Picra Spices, see page 18. Observing the precautions, as they are directed there, in all respects.

Section, 4.

****

Of CLYSTERS of various Sorts.

A Clyster for the STAGGERS.

TAKE two Bitter Apples and boil them in three quarts of Water for half an hour, then strain the liquor off, and add Sirup of Buckthron four ounces, and Sweet Oil half a pint. Repeat the above Clyster according as you see occasion require the use of them.

You

Of CLYSTERS.

You muſt obſerve in adminiſtering Clyſters, that your Clyſter-pipe is long and bulky, with a good Beef's bladder well tied to it; then if you can bear the bladder to your cheek in regard to heat, you may venture to adminiſter the Clyſter; but obſerve always, to have the Horſe to ſtand as high behind, and as low before as you can; as the Clyſter will operate beſt in that poſture; and alſo obſerve to keep the Clyſter in as long as you can, in order to drive it in or through the great gut, before it returns.

A Comfortable CLYSTER.

Take Bracken's Cordial Ball, four ounces, ſee page 28—diſſolved in two quarts of Watergruel; to which, add Sweet Oil two ounces, then for uſe; this is a ſafe and comfortable Clyſter; and will ſupport nature, in a long fatiguing illneſs; ſuch, as when the ſpirits are reduced quite low.

A Clyſter in a FEVER.

Take Sena one ounce and a half, and boil it in a quart of Water, then ſtrain it off; and to the decoction, add Common Treacle one pound, and Sweet Oil half a pint. This is a ſafe mild Clyſter, which may be repeated twice a-day; or as ſymptoms may require the uſe of it.

A Mild CLYSTER for a FOAL.

Take Common Treacle half a pint: Sweet Oil three ounces, and ſoft Water half a pint: diſſolve the whole together, and give it once a-day. The repetition of the above will ſoon relieve a Foal, that is coſtive, when young, or lately dropped.

The COLIC CLYSTER.

Take ſpring Water two quarts, Common Salt two large handfuls; or freſh-made Beef's Brine, of either, the ſame in quantity,

quantity, foft Soap four ounces and Goofe Oil half a pint; then fimmer all together over a flow fire for half an hour: then for ufe. The above Clyfter to be repeated in two hours time, if occafion may require the ufe of it.

A CLYSTER to Relax a Coftive Bowel.

Take the Urine of Cows, two or three quarts, whilft warm from the Cows, and adminifter the above as a Clyfter; and repeat the fame in three hours time, if needful, which will empty the Bowels plentifully with eafe.

A CLYSTER for an Inflammation in the Bowels.

Take Marfh Mallows, Common Mallows and Camomile Flowers or Herbs, of each a fingle handful; boil the whole in three quarts of Water: then add to the above; Annifeeds two ounces, Common Treacle half a pound and Sweet Oil half a pint. Repeat the above two or three times a-day, or as needful.

Always obferve to repeat bleeding, when there is an inflammation in the bowels.

An Aftringent CLYSTER.

Take Forge Water three quarts, Oak Bark four ounces, Tormentil Root two ounces, and Pomegranate Bark two ounces; boil the whole well together; then ftrain the decoction off; to which add Diafcordium two ounces, Mithridate one ounce, and the Tincture of Opium four drams: then mixed all together and given as a Clyfter, in a lax, or fcouring.

The above is very proper to be given as a drink; efpecially if the Clyfter is divided into three drinks, and given properly. This is an excellent medicine in the Bloody Flux; and will anfwer the whole of the above intention.

Section

Section 5.

Of PURGING PHYSIC of Various Sorts.

PHYSIC is very proper for Horfes that labour under diforders of feveral Sorts; as when the blood and juices are in a bad ftate or habit, or when the limbs and other vitals are become languid and gummy, and fhort of action or due circulation. Alfo, Purging Phyfic is very proper for Horfes that have high keep; fuch, as are in training, or hunters, hacks, and the like: nor can a man or groom bring a horfe properly into condition, without the help of Purging Phyfic; as when parts get languid and gummy, and fhort of action: then a dofe or two of Purging Phyfic will free the mufcles and fmall fibres, and fweeten the blood and juices, and caufe all parts to act according to their ufual and due circulation. When you mean to give Phyfic, firft take blood, and give him, for two or three days, Scalded Bran and Oats, to prepare his body properly for the reception of Phyfic: then make ufe of any of the following Purges; as fymptoms may require the ufe of them.

A Gentle Mild PURGE.

Take the beft Barbadoes Aloes one ounce, Spermaceti one dram, Caftile Soap one dram, Jalap half a dram, Race Ginger in powder, one dram, Diapente half an ounce, Salt of Tartar one dram, and Oil of Annifeed forty drops; made up in a ball with Sirup of Buckthorn for one dofe: to this and to all other Purges, I add more or lefs Aloes; according to the ftrength, or habit of the Horfe's body.

A Gentle

Of PURGES.

A Gentle Mild PURGE.

Take Barbadoes Aloes one ounce, Race Ginger two drams, Castile Soap one dram, Salt of Tartar one dram, all in fine powder, made up into a ball with Sirup of Buckthorn for one dose: if you should wish the above to act as an alterative; then, instead of one dram of Salt of Tartar, make use of four drams, to the above Purge; and then it will act as an alterative, and pass through the whole mass of Blood.

A Purge may work the first day it is given; but commonly not until the second day; although I have known a Purge to lay in a horse three days, and worked well off at last; however I will advise, not to stir a horse out of the stable but as little as possible whilst the physic is operating; but if necessity should urge, to give a horse a gentle turn out, in the time his physic is operating; let them be very short turns, not above half an hour at one time: for there is no need of exercise during the operation of physic, since every Purge will carry itself off, with keeping warm, and supplying the horse with warm Water or thin Watergruel; and that pretty often, but not above a quarter of a pailful at one time: and also, I do advise all grooms and keepers of horses, not to toil and fatigue a horse with exercise in the time of physic, but rub and whisp him well over and circulate him well in the stall. The above ill-practice of too severe exercise in physic, has been the death of several brave horses, to my certain knowledge. Also, I further say, if the horse works well in the stable, he need not be taken out at all, while the physic is operating; but if the physic does not work off well, let him have three or four turns out, in the space of the day, and not above half an hour at one time.

Another

Of PURGES.

Another Mild PURGE.

Take Barbadoes Aloes, from one ounce to ten drams, Spermaceti one dram, Diapente half an ounce, Caſtile Soap one dram, Salt of Tartar one dram, Race Ginger in Powder one dram, Myrrh one dram, Oil of Anniſeeds forty drops, made up into a ball with Sirup of Buckthorn, for one doſe, If the laſt Purges ſhould be required ſtronger, I ſometimes add Jalap one dram, or a dram and a half or two drams, more or leſs, according as it may be required.

A Strong Safe PURGE.

Take Barbadoes Aloes from one ounce to twelve drams, Spermaceti one dram, Cream of Tartar half an ounce, Jalap from one, to two drams, Race Ginger in powder one dram, Diapente half an ounce, Caſtile Soap two drams, and Oil of Anniſeeds forty drops; made up into two balls with Sirup of Buckthorn for one doſe. Sometimes I add to the above, inſtead of Jalap, one dram or two of Scammony, more or leſs, according to the ſtrength or habit of the Horſe's body. The above is not meant for a delicate habit, but a robuſt ſtrong habit, as ſome Horſes require Phyſic much ſtronger than others do. But let this be a rule, ſay you mean to give, one, two, or four doſes of Purging Phyſic to a Horſe; the firſt doſe might happen juſt to ſuit the habit and work well to your mind: Although you give juſt the ſame doſe again it might not work ſo well as the firſt did: alſo, I will adviſe to add a little more Aloes and Jalap to the ſecond and third doſes and ſo-forth, as generally the habit gets ſtronger and ſtronger after every doſe you give.

Of PURGES.

Physic commonly given to HORSES at GRASS.

Take Barbadoes Aloes, from seven to nine drams, Race Ginger in powder two drams, Spermaceti one dram, Diapente four drams; made up into a ball with Sirup of Buckthorn for one dose. The above will work off mild and easy, at Grass. The day you intend to give the above Physic, take the Horse up early that morning from Grass, and let him fast three hours, then give him the above Purge, and let him fast two hours after it; then let him eat Hay for two hours; afterwards give him a feed of Corn, and then turn him to Grass: so repeat another dose in five or six days after, or according as it has operated, and so-forth.

The Hiera Picra Spices, or the HOLY BITTER.

Take Cinnamon Bark, Mace, Snake Root, Gum Arabic, and Saffron, of each six drams; fine Barbadoes Liver Aloes one pound; all made into fine powder, mixed together and kept in a pot for use. This is a very safe Purge and may be given after a long sickness or illness, or any disorder whatever; and very proper to be given in a lingering gripe: the dose is from one ounce to two; more or less, as you see occasion; to be made up into a ball with Sirup of Buckthorn. It also may be given to a sucking Foal, that follows the Dam with safety: the dose to a Foal, is two or three drams given in half a pint of mild Ale, with three spoonfuls of Common Treacle, made warm together. The above is a good medicine to destroy Worms, and will cause a Foal to thrive well after it.

The SCOURING after a SWEAT.

Take Barbadoes Aloes, from six drams to one ounce, Castile Soap two drams, Bracken's Cordial Ball four drams, see page 28,

28, made up into a ball, with Sirup of Buckthorn, for one dose. Do not set the Horse on the muzzle for this Sweat, but let him walk and canter about for two hours; and then let him begin to Sweat; when that is over, let him be scraped clean and dry, and then give him three hornsuls of a comfortable drink prepared ready for that purpose. Then let him walk out for half an hour, or until he is quite dry and settled, then take him in and give him the scouring ball, then give him three hornfuls of the aforesaid cordial drink, and set him up fair: use him as if he was in physic for the two ensuing days; and so go on with him regular and easy in his exercise until such time he is fit to Sweat again; then do the same as before-mentioned, for three or four Sweats together. By the above method, I have kept several rheumatic crippled Racers sound, during the whole summer, which would not have stood if they had not been treated as above-mentioned.

A PURGE for the MOLTEN GREASE.

Take Glauber's Salts three ounces, Cream of Tartar two ounces, Lenitive Electuary three ounces, Nitre Salts one ounce, Salt of Tartar two drams, Treacle half a pound, Sweet Oil half a pint; given in a quart of Watergruel, for one dose. If given in the Staggers, I add Jalap three or four drams.— The above to be repeated every fifth or sixth day, or as occasion may require.

A Quick PURGE for an Inflamed BOWEL.

Take Lenitive Electuary three ounces, Salt of Tartar three drams, Glauber's Salts three ounces, Common Treacle one pound, and Sweet Oil half a pint; all dissolved in a pint of warm Ale for one dose. The above will pass mild and easy, and may be repeated in four days time, or according as fymptoms may require the ufe of it.

The Method of giving MERCURIAL PHYSIC.

Take Calomel that has often been fublimed from one dram to two, Diapente half an ounce, Bracken's Cordial Ball one ounce, fee page 28, made up into a ball, with Sirup of Marfh Mallows. Give the above at fix o'Clock in the Evening, fafting three hours before the ball is given, and let him faft three hours after it: give warm Water and Mafhes, and the next morning give him the following Purging Ball.

Take the fineft Barbadoes Aloes one ounce or ten drams, Spermaceti one dram, Diapente four drams, Myrrh in powder one dram, Saffron half a dram, Jalap one dram, Salt of Tartar one dram, and the Powers of Amber a tea-fpoonful: made up into a ball with Sirup of Marfh Mallows. Keep the Horfe warm and do not ftir him out in this Phyfic: give him warm Water and Mafhes, or dry Bran, and fweet Hay. Repeat the fame according as the Horfe recovers. Do not repeat the above dofe too foon; as Phyfic of this kind requires a Horfe to be well braced before it is repeated; that is to give proper interval between his Phyfic; I mean a fortnight at leaft.

An Aftringent PURGE for a LAX or SCOURING.

Take Barbadoes Aloes from fix to eight drams, Spermaceti one dram, Rhubarb half an ounce, Salt of Tartar two drams, Diapente four drams, Race Ginger in powder one dram, made up into a ball with Sirup of Buckthorn for one dofe: and to be repeated as occafion may require the ufe of it.

Of ALTERATIVE PURGES.

When a PURGE doth not work and caufes a Horfe to Swell.

Take one pint of Lifbon Wine, and mix with it one dram of Camphire, diffolved in a little Spirit of Wine, to which add Oil of Juniper two drams, the Powers of Amber two drams, Sirup of Marfh Mallows four ounces; give the above made warm as a drink: then ftir him about very gently, this will caufe him to pifs and empty himfelf plentifully. After the ufe of any of the above Purging Phyfic is over, and if the Phyfic has taken more hold than common; and has reduced the Horfe lower than you would wifh, then it will be proper to give him two or three Cordial Drinks to heal his Stomach, and revive his Spirits up again; at the fame time to give him Gum Arabic one ounce, diffolved in all his common Water; that is, one ounce a-day for a week together. After the ufe of the above, it would be very proper to indulge him with fome frefh Grafs, that is, to be led out in hand for an hour in the warmeft part of the day. Obferve to clothe him warm at all times whilft he is out in hand at Grafs.

Section 6.

Of ALTERATIVE PURGES.

NOTWITHSTANDING, that thefe kinds of Purges work much by excrement, but pafs through the whole mafs of blood, and refrefh the blood and juices in the whole frame, efpecially in foul grofs habits, fuch as Farcies and Surfeits, and foulnefs of the fkin. And the following method anfwers well to purge thick-winded Horfes, that are afflicted with old coughs and phthifics.

An *ALTERATIVE PURGE.*

Take fine Barbadoes Aloes, fix or eight drams, Spermaceti one dram, Cream of Tartar half an ounce, Diapente half an ounce, Jalap and Salt of Tartar of each one dram, Gum Guiacum one dram, Cinnabar of Antimony two drams, and the Powers of Amber a tea-fpoonful; made up into a ball with Sirup of Buckthorn, for one dofe: this to be given once a week, or according as it operates, or as neceffity may require the ufe of it.

An *ALTERATIVE PURGE.*

Take Lenitive Electuary eight ounces, Jalap and Scammony of each one ounce, Cinnabar of Antimony fix ounces, Gum Guiacum two ounces, Nitre Salts three ounces, and Camphire half an ounce; made up into eight balls with Sirup of Buckthorn: one of the above balls to be given every fifth day, or as they operate; they will work off mild and eafy, chiefly by urine, and may be given as fymptoms may require the ufe of them.

An *ALTERATIVE PURGE.*

Take Barbadoes Aloes, fix or eight drams, Spermaceti one dram, Gum Galbanum, Gum Ammoniacum, and Affafœtida, of each two drams, Diapente half an ounce, Saffron, half a dram, and Oil of Annifeeds forty drops, made up into a ball with Sirup of Buckthorn for one dofe. To be given according as they operate. The above Alteratives are proper to purge thick-winded and purfive Horfes: alfo are proper to be given in foulnefs of the fkin, as they moftly go off by urine.

Section,

Section, 7.

Of ALTERATIVE BALLS.

THE operation of the following Balls is to sweeten the blood and juices; as they are very proper to be given when physic cannot be administered; as when parts get viscid gummy or sizy, and short of true circulation; which often occasions lameness, in several parts of the body. They wholly go off by urine, and are of great service to dim eyes; and require no confinement, nor particular diet. They generally bring a Horse very fresh and fine in his coat or skin, and will refresh the whole mass of blood.

The ALTERATIVE BALLS.

Take Castile Soap one pound, Salt of Prunella half a pound, Stone Brimstone in fine powder four ounces, White Rosin in fine powder four ounces, Balsam of Sulphur drawn with Oil of Turpentine two ounces, Liver of Antimony in fine powder eight ounces, Cinnabar of Antimony in fine powder six ounces, Gum Guiacum two ounces, Honey four ounces, made up into a ball with Flour of Brimstone for use. One large ball or two small ones to be given for one dose; the above balls may be given every other day, or rather after a hard day's work, such as after a sweat, or a day's hunting or the like.

Another ALTERATIVE BALL.

Take Cinnabar of Antimony, and Gum Guiacum, of each, in fine powder half a pound, Castile Soap half a pound, Flour of Brimstone one pound, Diapente six ounces, Salt of Tartar
four

four ounces, Nitre Salts half a pound, and Camphire one ounce and a half, made up into a ball with Honey and Annifeeds in powder for ufe. The dofe is a moderate fized ball, to be given every other day; repeat ten of the above balls. The above are very proper for Horfes that are fubject to moving lamenefs, that is firft in one part and then in another; at the fame time bleed every fortnight, to affift and thin the blood. This and the former ball are very proper for Horfes in training, that are fubject to moving lamenefs: as running Horfes are obliged to go through a vaft deal of hardfhip and fatigue in all their exercifes. If the Horfe is any way able to go on with his work, give him two fmall balls after every fweat, and two fmall balls between each fweat. The above method, if properly obferved, will keep a cripple firm, frefh and bloomy.

A Valuable ALTERATIVE for the whole Mafs of Blood.

Take Crocus Metallorum, or the Liver of Antimony, of either one pound, in perfect fine powder. Give of either of the above, one ounce, or one ounce and a half, once a-day in a Mafh of Bran and Oats, for a fortnight together: but if the above fhould caufe a Purging; make ufe of the above once every other day. The above reftores a loft Appetite, and kills Worms; purifies the Blood, by removing Obftructions, and fattens tired and wafted Horfes.

The Alterative MINERAL BALL.

Take Turbith Mineral half a dram, Caftile Soap half an ounce, Diapente half an ounce, made up into a ball with Honey for one dofe. The above is an excellent medicine for fweetening the blood and juices; to be given every other day;

for

Of ALTERATIVE BALLS.

for a week or ten days: and alfo, is proper to be made ufe of, when a Horfe has met with a very fevere wound; it forwards a cure, and brings on a good digeftion, when the body is in a bad habit. I have given the above Ball to Horfes at Grafs, when neceffity obliged me and it anfwered the purpofe well.

The Alterative MERCURIAL BALL, for a Scorbutic Itching and Scrubbing.

Take of the beft Pewter three ounces, and melt it in a pan, when melted, add to it, Quickfilver two ounces; then let it fimmer together for four minutes and ftir it with a wooden fplint all the while; then let it ftand until its quite cold, then make all in fine powder, in a mortar; then add Caftile Soap two ounces, Diapente two ounces, all mixed together and made up into a ball with Honey; then divide the whole into four dofes, one of which give, every fourth morning, fafting four hours before each dofe, and four hours after. Keep him warm, and give warm Water and Mafhes, during the time he has the balls, then reft a week; then repeat the fame as above directed; ftrictly obferving not to ftir him out during the time, thefe balls are given; but may have gentle exercife the week the balls are not given.

A Powerful ALTERATIVE MEDICINE, for a Lamenefs that moves from one Part to another like Rheumatifm.

Take Flour of Brimftone, from half a pound to one pound, and give it all at one time on a Mafh of Bran and Oats, if the Horfe will eat it, but if not, make the whole into balls with Treacle, and give all at one time, fafting. The above will open his body much; keep warm, and do not ftir out for fix

Of PISSING BALLS.

or eight days; then in twelve days time repeat the above, and use the same precautions as before directed; but first take blood, and be sure to keep warm.

Section, 8.

Of PISSING BALLS and DRINKS.

THE following Balls and Drinks, are wholly to check sharp humours, and to carry them off by the way of urine; and may be given to Horses of gross habits, that are subject to swelled legs and the like: also, are very proper to be given to Horses after they are stopped in the time of physic, when a humour remains, and is dropped down to the legs, and are very proper to be given to assist the cure of the Grease, and are very active in carrying off sharp humours by the way of urine.

A Mild PISSING BALL.

Take Diapente, Turmeric, Flour of Brimstone, Nitre Salt, Liver of Antimony of each half an ounce, White Rosin one ounce, Barbadoes Tar two drams; make the above into a ball with Honey for one dose; or may be divided for two doses, or give a moderate sized ball every other day, or according as they operate.

A Strong PISSING BALL.

Take Salt of Prunella, Salt of Tartar, Oil of Juniper, and Castile Soap of each one ounce, and White Rosin three ounces. Make the above into a ball with Diapente, Turmeric and Flour

Flour of Brimstone. One small ball to be given as you see occasion requires, or according as they operate.

The Genuine PISSING BALL.

Take Castile Soap three ounces, Balsam of Sulphur drawn with Oil of Turpentine, two ounces, Salt of Prunella four ounces, Æthiops Mineral two ounces, White Rosin six ounces, Liver of Antimony four ounces, Salt of Tartar one ounce, Flour of Brimstone six ounces, Honey three meat-spoonfuls and two large heads of Garlic; made up into a ball with Diapente and Turmeric for use: give two small balls for one dose, or, as you see occasion may require the use of them.

A PISSING DRINK.

Take White Rosin in powder three ounces, Honey two ounces, the Powers of Amber two drams, and Oil of Olives one ounce. Slice two large Onions into a quart of Ale overnight, the next morning strain it off; then add the above to the Ale, and give it for a Drink, fasting. The above is a very powerful drier of sharp humours in the cure of the Grease; and to be given as you see occasion may require the use of it.

Another PISSING DRINK.

Take Yellow Rosin, in fine powder three ounces, Salt of Prunella one ounce, Flour of Brimstone two ounces and the Powers of Amber two drams, all mixed together in a mortar, and given in a quart of Forge Water cold, for one dose. The above Balls and Drinks are powerful diuretics, and are great cleansers of the urinary Passage. To be given as symptoms may require the use of them: but observe, not to crowd the Animal with them too often, but give time for every dose to operate, before they are repeated. These diuretic medicines, go off very sharp by urine; and if a Horse is overcrowded with them, they will rack him much, and so bring on a Diabetes.

Section 9.

Of Cordial BALLS and Cordial DRINKS of various Sorts.

First of BRACKEN's Cordial BALL.

TAKE Anniseeds, Carraway Seeds, and Greater Cardamoms and Gentian in fine powder, of each two ounces, Flour of Brimstone four ounces, Turmeric four ounces, Diapente four ounces, Saffron four drams, Sugar Candy one pound, Spanish Juice dissolved in Hyssop Water four ounces, Liquorice Powder four ounces, Oil of Anniseeds two ounces, Honey half a pound, Sweet Oil one pint, Wheat Flour, a sufficient quantity to make the whole into a ball; by beating the above well together in a mortar for use. This ball has undergone some alterations of mine, since it has been in my practice.

For Fresh-taken COLDS.

For Fresh-taken Colds, observe to bleed in the first stage, then proceed as follows. Take of the above Cordial Ball, the size of a Hen's Egg, and dissolve it in a quart of warm Ale, to which add Camphire two drams, and Saffron half a dram; then mixed together for one dose and given every other day: two of the above Drinks are sufficient for any Fresh Cold.

Let

Of CORDIAL DRINKS.

Let this be a rule to all Men that adminifter Drinks to Horfes, to be duly careful in giving them, and not to cram great full hornfuls at once; and at the fame time not to check and keep their heads too high and force the Drink down by compulfion: as I may juftly fay, that if the Drink is ever fo mild, and two fpoonfuls or lefs, fhould happen to go down the wrong paffage, which is the windpipe, you may depend upon it to be certain death. Therefore let me advife the reader, that when he intends to give a Drink to let it be given in a fmall horn, and that not above half full at once; and if the Animal fhould cough, or ftruggle againft the Drink, let his Head down immediately and give him time to recover before any more is given him.

A Mollifying DRINK *for a* COLD.

Take Sirup of Horehound, Sirup of Garlic and Sirup of Coltsfoot of each two ounces, Sweet Oil one ounce, Spanifh Juice two ounces, Mithridate, Liquorice Powder, Flour of Brimftone, Diapente and Turmeric of each one ounce: then divided for two Drinks, and given in a quart of warm Ale. This Drink is very foft and mellow in its operation, to be given every other day. Two of the above Drinks feldom fail to cure a Frefh Cold, if given as above directed.

A DRINK *for a tired Horfe, after a hard Day's Work.*

Take of Bracken's Cordial Ball four ounces, Camphire four drams, mixed in a mortar together. Diffolve the above in a quart of warm Ale, and give it for one Drink. The above is very proper to be given to a Horfe or a Colt, that has taken Cold after Cutting; keep him warm after the above Drink.

The above will caufe a ftrong Sweat. The above Drink might be repeated in five days time, if occafion be.

A Searching

Of CORDIAL DRINKS.

A Searching Thriving DRINK.

Take Rue and Hyſſop of each a ſmall handful, a moderate ſized head of Garlic picked clean and bruiſed in a mortar, and Honey three ounces: boil the whole well together in a quart of Ale; then cover it up and let it ſtand all night; the next morning add Diapente, Turmeric, Liquorice Powder, and Flour of Brimſtone, of each one ounce, and Sweet Oil two ounces, all mixed together for one doſe, and to be given every other morning. This is a good Drink after a fatigue or hardſhip and will cauſe a Horſe to thrive well after it. Repeat three of the above Drinks.

Alſo, a DRINK for a tired Hunter, that has been deprived of all his Actions.

Take a full quart of Red Port Wine; make the above warm, then add the Tincture of Opium five drams; then ſtir the above well together, and give it as a Drink, as ſoon as poſſible. The above Drink will revive him much by morning, then uſe him moderately in his exerciſe.

BALLS for an INTERMITTING or SWEATING AGUISH Diſorder.

Take Gentian four ounces, Myrrh and Roch Allum of each two ounces, Galingal Root one ounce, Cinnamon Bark half an ounce, Saffron and Camphire of each three drams, Race Ginger one ounce, all in fine powder. Make the whole into a ball with Honey and divided into ſix balls; one of which give every morning, faſting: then omit the above balls for a week or ten days, then repeat the ſame again in all reſpects.

A DRINK

Of CORDIAL DRINKS.

A DRINK to Reſtore a loſt Appetite.

Take Bracken's Cordial Ball one ounce and a half, ſee page 28, diſſolved in a quart of warm Ale, then add Elixir of Vitriol one dram, and Diapente one ounce, mixed together for one doſe: to be repeated as occaſion may require the uſe of it.

The Aromatic Herbs DRINK.

Take Rue, Mint, Hyſſop, St. John's Wort, Agrimony, Valerian, Pennyroyal, Salandine, Garmandre, Roſemary, the Flowers and Tops of Marſh Mallows, and Roman Wormwood, of each a large double handful, chopped ſmall and dried, and kept cloſe for uſe, and when uſed, take a ſingle handful of the above Herbs, all mixed together, and two ounces of Juniper Berries, in powder, and a ſingle handful of Common Salt; then give the whole in a quart of warm Ale, for one drink, and repeat it four mornings together.—Firſt bleed.

The above is a valuable Drink, when you are not certain of the diſorder.

A DRINK to Strengthen the STOMACH and to cauſe an APPETITE.

Take Gentian Root ſliced thin one ounce, and Snake Root half an ounce; ſimmer the above in a quart of Water until it conſumes it to a pint: then cover it up all night; the next morning ſtrain it off, and add to the decoction Cochineal and Saffron, of each one dram, White Wine half a pint and Honey three meat ſpoonfuls; then boil the whole together, and give it faſting, for one doſe. This will ſoon bring a Horſe to his Appetite if repeated every other day: give three of the above Drinks.

Of OLD COUGHS.

The ANODYNE BALSAM.

Take Castile Soap two ounces, Gum Opium two ounces, Camphire one ounce, Saffron three drams, Oil of Rosemary six drams, Rectified Spirits of Wine eighteen ounces; put the whole into a quart bottle; digest the whole together, in a hot horse-dunghill, for six or eight days, shaking the bottle every day; then for use.

The above is an excellent Medicine to ease pain; such as in the Cholic, or any griping pain in the Bowels, or in the Staggers, or in any inward severe pain. The dose is half an ounce of the Anodyne Balsam; might be given in any mild cordial drink, or might be added to one ounce and a half of my Mithridate, for one drink.

Section 10.

Of BALLS and DRINKS to Relieve Old COUGHS and PHTHISICS.

OBSERVE in the above case to bleed, that is pretty often, once a fortnight at the least. Also Rowels and Issues are very proper to assist old Coughs and Phthisics, by repeating them for some time with the help of the following Medicines.

For a COUGH on a YOUNG HORSE.

Take a pint of common Eating Salt, and a pint of Spring Water; mix them together in a mortar until they are incorporated; then give the whole as a drink for one dose: to be repeated four or five mornings together. The above drink
seems

Of OLD COUGHS.

seems but simple, but is of great service to young Colts, as it is very offensive to worms and so-forth.

A DRINK to Relieve Old COUGHS.

Take a moderate sized head of Garlic, picked clean, bruise the Cloves in a mortar, then boiled in three half pints of Skim Milk, with three meat-spoonfuls of Honey, Annifeeds in powder two ounces, and give the whole for one dose, fasting: walk the Horse out for an hour after each drink. Repeat the above every morning for a fortnight together, at the same time take a quart of blood from him every week, or as occasion be. The above will prevent a Horse to become broken-winded, if given in proper time.

For a GROUNDED COUGH.

Take one pint of cold-drawn Linseed Oil, and two large heads of Garlic picked clean and pounded in a mortar; mix them together for one drink; give three of the above drinks, one every fourth day. At the same time you are to sprinkle all his Corn and Mashes with the Mullen Powder, for three weeks together. The Mullen Powder is prepared as follows: take of the Herb Mullen in fine powder one pound, Elecampane in powder one pound, and Gentian four ounces, mixed all together for use. This method being taken, will cure most Old Coughs whatever.

A DRINK for a GROUNDED COUGH.

Take Turmeric, Diapente, Liquorice Powder and Barbadoes Tar, of each one ounce, Grains of Paradise, and Balsam of Sulphur drawn with Oil of Turpentine, of each half an ounce, Oil of Annifeeds half an ounce, Elecampane three ounces,

Of OLD COUGHS.

ounces, Honey two meat-spoonfuls, and two large heads of Garlic bruised in a mortar; all mixed together, and divided for two drinks, to be given in a quart of warm Ale: at the same time give a small handful of Linseed upon every Feed of Corn and Mash you give, for three weeks together or longer. Repeat six of the above drinks, one every other day. This method seldom fails to cure a bad Cough or Phthisic.

The TAR BALLS for Old COUGHS.

Take Flour of Brimstone, Album Græcum, Liquorice Powder, and Elecampane, of each four ounces, Balsam of Sulphur drawn with Oil of Turpentine three ounces, and Barbadoes Tar five ounces; made up into balls with the Mullen Powder, see page 33. Give a moderate sized ball every morning, fasting, before his exercise, for eight mornings together.

The GUM BALLS for Old COUGHS.

Take Gum Ammoniacum, Gum Galbanum, Assafœtida and Balsam of Sulphur drawn with Oil of Turpentine, of each two ounces, Cinnabar of Antimony six ounces, Venice Turpentine three ounces, Saffron half an ounce, Garlic four ounces, and Honey eight ounces: made up into a ball with Flour of Brimstone and Elecampane. Give a moderate sized ball every morning, fasting, for ten days together. Then omit giving the balls for ten or twelve days, then repeat the same again. The above methods properly observed will get clear of Old Coughs, but observe to bleed once a week; the first time you bleed take two quarts or better, and after, in small quantities not to exceed a quart at a time, except the blood appears to be bad, then you must take a greater quantity; so continue bleeding until you see the blood to be of a due consistence and clear from size.

Section,

Section, 11.

Of a RATTLING and Stoppage in the HEAD and a Running at the NOSE.

THE symptoms of the above disorder are, when a Horse is pressed or fatigued more than common, he will Rattle in the Head and Glands; and will run at the Nose, a slimy matter, which causes some people to think, and say, that such Horses are glandered; but I answer no, it is a superfluous phlegmatic humour that lodges upon the Glands of some gross pursive Horses: Therefore make use as follows. Observe in the above case to bleed often, that is, once a fortnight at least, so, continue bleeding until you find the blood to be of a due consistence: at the same time give the following ball.

A BALL for a RATTLING in the HEAD.

Take Matthew's Pill three or four drams, Elecampane one ounce and a half, and Bracken's Cordial Ball one ounce, see page 28, mix them together for one dose. Give one of these balls every morning fasting, for a fortnight together; and give moderate exercise during the whole time.

MATTHEW's PILL.

Matthew's Pill is prepared as follows; take the Extract of Opium, Black Hellebore, Liquorice Powder, and Soap of Tartar, of each four ounces, and Saffron four drams, beat them all well together in a mortar, and mix them up into a ball with Balsam of Sulphur drawn with Oil of Turpentine: then for use.

Of a RATTLING in the HEAD.

The TAR-WATER DRINK for a Rattling in the HEAD, and a Running at the NOSE.

Take common clean Tar two pounds, spring Water three quarts, mix the whole together in a narrow throated jug with a stick for use. Give one quart of the above Water when clear, for one drink, in a morning fasting; and repeat the same every morning for a fortnight together: walk the Animal out for an hour after each drink; and as you take one quart out of the jug for use, put in one quart of fresh Water, stirring it well together; the Tar will serve for all the while.

For a WHEEZING in the STOMACH.

Take the Wine of Squills four ounces, Liquorice Stick in powder one ounce and a half, Anniseeds one ounce and a half bruised, mix the whole in one quart of Watergruel that has been well boiled and strained; give the above fasting, for one dose, and repeat the same twice a week, or as necessity urges. The repetition of the above will free the Stomach much. I have prepared the Wine of Squills as follows.

Take Sea Onions bruised eight ounces, and infuse them in two quarts of strong Stale Beer, which answers the same purpose as the above Wine of Squills.

The NOSE DRINK for the same.

Take White Wine Vinegar and White Wine of each half a pint, fine Tobacco, Roch Allum and Rosemary, of each one ounce, Saffron half an ounce all in fine powder, and Honey of Roses two ounces, all mixed, and simmered together over a slow fire: then strained, and bottled for use. Give of the above, a meat-spoonful down each Nostril, in a morning fasting, before his exercise.

Section,

Section, 12.

Of DRINKS to Promote PERSPIRATION.

TAKE Mithridate two ounces, and diffolve it in a quart of warm Ale; then add to it, one ounce and a half of Tincture of Saffron and Camphire, fee the bottom of this page: mix all together, then add Common Treacle one pound, for one dofe. If it fhould be thought neceffary for a Horfe to be continued in his Sweat; repeat the above drink according as fymptoms may require the ufe of it, that is, every fourth day.

A DRINK to Promote SWEAT.

Take green Bark of fmall Twigs of Oak, a large handful, and boil it in two quarts of Ale until it is near half confumed; then ftrain it, then add Common Treacle one pound, and give it as a drink. This will caufe a ftrong Sweat: keep warm with clothes and encourage the Sweat. Repeat it as you fee occafion.

The former of the two laft receipts is proper to be given in Malignant and Peftilent Fevers: and as I have not fet down how to prepare the Tincture of Saffron and Camphire it is as follows.

The Tincture of SAFFRON and CAMPHIRE.

Take the beft rectified Spirits of Wine one pint, Saffron chopped fmall fix drams, and Camphire two ounces; mix them all together for ufe, when ufed, the dofe is three meatfpoonfuls, or five might be given in high violent fits of the

Staggers or Fevers: in the firſt ſtage if very wild, add to the above Tincture, Mithridate two ounces and a half, and Tincture of Opium two drams; mix them together and let it be given in a quart of ſmall Ale: and as I obſerved before in the Section, of the Staggers to take blood plentifully, that is, three or four quarts at one time.

Section 13.

Of DRINKS for SUDDEN ACCIDENTS,

THAT cauſe pain in the Bowels, from being overthrown in a wet ditch, or the like, or by the ill effect of a bad damp ſtable, or the ill-treatment of a groom or ſuch like man, that has given cold Water, when the body was hot and empty: alſo from a houſe-ſervant that rides a Horſe to a public-houſe door, then turns the poor creature into the yard, with a ſtroke from his whip; then it is a good ten to one, but the Horſe goes to the ciſtern of Water, and drinks to ſuch a degree that he is liable to catch his death or the like malady. In ſuch caſes make uſe, as follows. Take Matthew's Pill four drams, ſee page 35, Mithridate two ounces, Saffron one dram, Camphire two drams and a half: mix them all together, and diſſolve them in a quart of ſtrong Beer; then add Common Treacle half a pound, for one doſe. This will ſweat him much; keep him warm and encourage the ſweat. The above to be repeated as occaſion may require the uſe of it.

A DRINK for SUDDEN ACCIDENTS.

Take Bracken's Cordial Ball two ounces, ſee page 28, Mithridate one ounce, Saffron one dram, Camphire three drams,

the

Of BODY STRAINS.

the Powers of Amber a meat-fpoonful, and Common Treacle half a pound: diffolve the whole in a quart of ftrong Beer for one dofe. If the pain in the bowels fhould continue, and the fweating abate, after the effect of the above drink; you muft then repeat the drink and encourage the fweat until fuch time the pain abates. Should an inflammation in the bowels arife from the above complaint, it will be proper to bleed, and give the Clyfter for an Inflammation in the Bowels, fee page 14. The Clyfter is to be repeated three times a-day; then give the Quick Purge for an Inflamed Bowel, fee page 19, as they are recommended there in all refpects.

Section, 14.

Of BODY STRAINS.

THE fymptoms of a Body Strain are as follow; a Horfe will be ftiff in his Body, and fore in all his whole frame, and will fet his back up, perching with his four feet and legs, tucked up all together, when he ftands; and will be ftiff and painful, and rather drag his hind toes, and his belly tucked up to his back, with a ftaring coat, with a lofs of appetite; and will appear very unfit for any kind of bufinefs whatever. Firft bleed, then make ufe of the following drink.

For a BODY STRAIN.

Take Mithridate two ounces, Matthew's Pill four drams, fee page 35, Camphire two drams, Saffron one dram, Bracken's Cordial Ball two ounces, fee page 28, Tincture of Cantharides

one

one tea-spoonful, dissolve the whole in a quart of warm Ale for one dose. Give one of the above drinks, every other day, or as occasion may require the use thereof.

A DRINK for a BODY STRAIN.

Take Isinglass two ounces chopped small, then boiled in two quarts of Ale until its consumed to a quart; then add Venice Turpentine two ounces, Balsam of Sulphur drawn with Oil of Turpentine one ounce, Mithridate two ounces, Juniper Berries two ounces, and Carraway Seeds one ounce, mixed all together and divided for two doses: give one of these drinks every other day. After the repetition of either of the above drinks, it would be proper to add a gentle alterative purge or two, in the recovery of the above disorder; I will recommend the Hiera Picra Spices, see page 18, and to make use of them as they are recommended there in all respects.

Section, 15.

Of a LAX or SCOURING.

IN a Lax, never stop it in its first stage but rather encourage it, as it may proceed from a cold, or from some unwholesome food, or the like; or may come on from some ill sharp juices in the stomach; therefore never stop a Lax at the first; then make use of the following Purge.

A QUICK PURGE for a LAX.

Take Lenitive Electuary, and Cream of Tartar, of each two ounces, Yellow Rosin one ounce, the Powers of Amber a meat-spoonful, meat-spoonful, Sweet Oil two ounces, and Common Treacle half a pound, all diffolved together in a quart of Ale; do not put the Rofin in until the above are all diffolved together, and ftood until cold; then put the Rofin in, and ftir them all together for one dofe. Repeat the above as occafion may require the ufe thereof.

A PURGE for a LAX.

Take Barbadoes Aloes fix drams, Spermaceti one dram, Rhubarb four drams, Myrrh one dram, Saffron one dram, and Oil of Annifeeds forty drops; made up into a ball with Sirup of Buckthorn, for one dofe. This may be repeated once a week, or as fymptoms may require the ufe of it; then after it make ufe of the following Aftringent Drink.

An ASTRINGENT DRINK for a LAX.

Take a handful of Oak Bark, Tormentil-root one ounce, Roch Allum fix drams, boil them in two quarts of Forge Water until it is confumed to a quart; then odd Diafcordium one ounce and a half, Starch two ounces, Tincture of Opium two drams and mix them all together for one dofe: to be repeated as occafion may require the ufe of it; or you may make ufe of the following Clyfter or Drink.

An ASTRINGENT CLYSTER or DRINK.

Take Oak Bark four ounces, Tormentil-root two ounces, Pomegranate Bark and Red Rofes dried, of each a fmall handful; boil the above in four quarts of Forge Water until it is confumed to two quarts; then add Diafcordium two ounces, Mithridate one ounce and a half, and Tincture of Opium two drams, give the above as a Clyfter. This will ftop the Bloody

Of a LAX.

Flux if given as a drink, especially if it is divided for three drinks, and repeated once a-day for three or four days: at the same time make use of the above Clyster if occasion may require the use of it.

A Mellow Softening DRINK in a LAX.

Take Isinglass two ounces, chopped small, and boiled in three pints of Sweet Milk, over a slow Fire until thoroughly mixed; give the whole as a drink in a morning fasting.— Repeat the above drink for four or five mornings together. The above is valuable when the Stomach and Bowels are galled; and also, is of great use in the shedding of Nature.

For a LOOSENESS on a FOAL that follows the DAM.

Take a double handful of Gorse Blossoms, and boil them in two quarts of Sweet Milk: give three small hornfuls of the above three or four times a-day, until braced, or as long as occasion may require the use of it.

To Stop a LAX or SCOURING.

Take a Sheet of coarse Brown Paper and pound it in a mortar, with as much Water as will somewhat wet it; pound it all to a chyle, then add one quart of Ale to the above; then mix it all together: make it warm, and give it for one drink; and repeat it as occasion may require the use of it.

To Stop OVER-PURGING to Excess in the Time of PHYSIC.

Take Red Port Wine one quart, Soft Water one quart, Loaf Sugar four ounces, Cinnamon Bark, Cloves, Mace, and Nutmeg, of each two drams, in powder: boil the above over a slow fire; then add as much old White Bread as will thicken

the

Of the COLIC.

the whole for ufe. Give two or three hornfuls of this cordial, three or four times a-day. To be repeated as occafion may require the ufe of it.

To Stop OVER-PURGING in the Time of PHYSIC.

Take Diapente one ounce, Myrrh two drams, Saffron one dram, and Tincture of Opium two drams; put the above in a pint of Red Port Wine, and warm the whole together for one dofe: to be repeated once a-day if occafion may require the ufe of it.

When a LAX or SCOURING has continued a long Time, and has Galled and Fretted the Membrane of the GUT, I would advife to make ufe, as follows.

Take Gum Arabic two ounces, Ifinglafs two ounces fhred and chopped fmall, and Starch half a pound, boil them together in five quarts of Water, until they are diffolved: then let the Horfe have a quart of the above Water, mixed with his common Water, three times a-day, for nine days or a fortnight together at leaft.

Section, 16.

Of the COLIC or GRIPES.

THE firft fymptoms of the Colic are thefe; a Horfe will hang down his head in the manger and look dull foon after, will heave and pant at the flank much, and feem to be in a cold fweat: then will become very reftlefs and turn his head to his fide; and will lie down and tumble over and over; and

and will lie on his back by choice, and will not reſt in any other poſture whatever: his ears will be in a cold ſweat during the time the pain continues.

In the firſt ſymptoms of the Colic, give as follows, then I ſay, firſt bleed and take near three quarts; catch one quart of the Blood, and immediately add to the Blood, one ſingle handful of Common Salt, and ſtir it well together, and give it as a drink. The above ſeldom fails, but if it fails, then give either of the four following Receipts.

For the COLIC or GRIPES, of the dry Kind.

Take the Powers of Amber two drams, Venice Turpentine and Juniper Berries of each one ounce, Salt of Prunella half an ounce, Spermaceti two drams, Oil of Juniper one dram, Salt of Tartar two drams, make the whole into a ball with Sirup of Marſh Mallows for one doſe. If the above doth not ſucceed in two hours, repeat the ſame again; diſſolve the above ball in a pint of warm Ale. Firſt bleed and rake him, and empty the great gut; then immediately give the Colic Clyſter, ſee page 13.

For the DRY GRIPES.

Take Juniper Berries two ounces, Anniſeeds one ounce, Grains of Paradiſe two drams, make all the above in fine Powder, Salt of Tartar three drams, Hollands Gin half a pint, Sweet Oil four ounces. Give the whole in a pint of warm Ale for one doſe.

For the DRY GRIPES.

Take Tincture of Opium and Oil of Juniper of each half an ounce, Salt of Tartar three drams, Friar's Balſam one ounce; Grains of Paradiſe two drams, in fine Powder, Sweet Oil four ounces,

Of the COLIC.

ounces; then diffolve the fame in a pint of warm Ale, for one dofe; then rake him, and immediately give the Colic Clyfter, fee page 13. The above to be repeated in two hours time, if occafion may require the ufe of it.

For the DRY GRIPES.

Firft bleed and rake him, and empty the great Gut. Then take Spring Water one pint, Common Salt two full fingle handfuls, and Soft Soap three ounces; let the whole fimmer over a flow fire for half an hour; then add Sweet Oil fix ounces, then for ufe. Give the above for one drink, and immediately after, give the Colic Clyfter, fee page 13, this feldom or ever fails a cure if given as above directed. In a violent fevere Colic, I add to the above Colic drink, Tincture of Opium half an ounce.

A new Method for the GRIPES.

Firft bleed, then take a quart of Spring Water that has been ftrongly fmoked with Tobacco Smoke, and give it as a drink; this will caufe a ftrong fweat, clothe warm. The above Water is prepared in the following manner. Take a quart of Spring Water and put it into a large quart bottle; then fill a pipe full of Tobacco and fire it, then put the fhank of the pipe into the bottom of the bottle, then put another pipe's fhank into the bottle, but not fo deep as to reach the Water by three inches; then let the neck of the bottle be clofe luted up with Dough or Clay, and then fmoke away. The fmoke will draw through the Water. The faid bottle of Water fhould have five or fix pipes full of Tobacco fmoked through it, before it is fit for ufe. It would be proper to have two or three bottles of this Water prepared ready, and corked up clofe for ufe.

Of the COLIC.

For the WET GRIPES with a PURGING.

Take Diapente one ounce, Diafcordium one ounce, Myrrh two drams, Camphire two drams, and the Powers of Amber one meat-fpoonful; made up into an Electuary with Sirup of Marfh Mallows; diffolve the whole in a quart of warm Ale for one dofe. To be repeated as occafion may require the ufe of it.

For a SCOURING in a Lingering GRIPE.

Take Sena half an ounce, and boil it in a quart of Water for half an hour; then ftrain it off and add Salt of Tartar half an ounce, Lenitive Electuary two ounces, Glauber's Salts two ounces, and Sweet Oil four ounces. Give the above for one dofe; to be repeated every fourth day, or according as occafion may require the ufe of it.

For a Lingering GRIPE, with a Stiffnefs in the BODY.

Take Mithridate two ounces, Matthew's Pill three drams, fee page 35, Camphire two drams diffolved in a little Spirits of Wine, Saffron chopped fmall one dram, and Bracken's Cordial Ball two ounces, fee page 28. Diffolve the above in a quart of warm Ale for one dofe. Give the above drink every other day, or as occafion may require the ufe of it.

For a Lingering GRIPE, that is attended with a LAX.

Take Rhubarb one ounce, Salt of Tartar three drams, Race Ginger in Powder two drams, Bracken's Cordial Ball two ounces, fee page 28, Mithridate one ounce, Tincture of Opium three drams. Diffolve the above in a quart of warm Ale for one dofe. This to be repeated every fourth day or as occafion may require the ufe of it.

Of the PLEURISY.

If the GRIPES should Continue

A long time, and the Excrement or Stools seem to look of a black colour, and stink much, and are oft repeated in small quantities; it seems then to be dangerous, and a great appearance of a mortification coming on. In the above case I would advise to make use of all the Cooling Clysters, see page 14, and throw them up often, that is twice or thrice a day; likewise, to make use of the Cooling Quick Purge, see page 19. And at the same time to boil with all the Water he has, a double handful of Marsh Mallows and Parsley, to which add one ounce of Gum Arabic dissolved in a pint of hot Water, and mixed with all his common Water; that is one ounce a-day mixed with the Decoction of Mallows and Parsley, which is for his common drinking.

Section, 17.

Of the PLEURISY and INFLAMMATION of the LUNGS.

IN this disorder a Horse shews great uneasiness; he often strives to lay down, but starts up again immediately, then will turn his head to his side. The above symptoms has caused several men to mistake the Pleurisy, and think it to be the Gripes. In a Gripe a Horse lays down, and rolls and tumbles himself over and over, and afterwards lays on his back by his own choice; but in a Pleurisy there are no such symptoms; for a Horse in a Pleurisy has his ears and feet always hot, and his mouth dry, and seems much in a Fever, and generally has

a short

Of the PLEURISY.

a short Cough. In the first place bleed, and immediately put in two or three Rowels, then give him soft Emollient Clysters; repeat the bleeding, and the Clysters if needful. Then give as follow.

An ELECTUARY for the PLEURISY.

Take Spermaceti, Nitre Salt, and Comfrey-root, of each one ounce, Oil of Annifeeds, half an ounce, made up into an Electuary with Sirup of Marsh Mallows for one dose. Give one dose of the above every day, or according as symptoms may require the use of them. Dissolve the above in a quart of Watergruel.

A DECOCTION for the PLEURISY.

Take Marsh Mallows, Common Mallows and Comfrey-root or Herb, of each a large handful, Fenugreek bruised one pound, and Linseed one pound, boil the above in a small boiler full of Water, and let the Horse have this sort of Water for his common drinking, during his whole illness.

A DRINK for the PLEURISY.

Take Colts-foot and Ground-ivy, of each a large handful, Garlic and Horse-radish, of each two ounces, and Saffron two drams: boil the whole in four quarts of Water; then add cold-drawn Linseed Oil half a pint, and Common Treacle one pound; all simmered together over a slow fire, for use, then give of the above one quart once a-day or as symptoms may require the use of it.

The Bathing SPIRIT in the PLEURISY.

Take Spirits of Sal Ammoniac, and Oil of Camomile of each the same quantity, mixed together for use, rub and bathe the ribs

ribs and cheſt with the above once a-day, and continue rubbing until the pain abates. Then make uſe of the following cooling purge, if there be occaſion for it. Take Lenitive Electuary three ounces, Glauber's Salts three ounces, Cream of Tartar two ounces, Common Treacle one pint, and Sweet Oil half a pint, for one doſe, given in a pint of warm Ale. The above to be repeated in four days time, if neceſſity ſhould require the uſe of it.

Section 18.

Of HURTS in the KIDNEYS, and GRAVEL in the Parts thereof.

THE ſymptoms of a Hurt and Gravel in the Kidneys, and Bladder, are a weakneſs in the back and loins, and in pain when he piſſes; and when he doth piſs, it is muddy and thick with ſtreaks of blood, and ſometimes all blood, with a loſs of appetite and a ſtaring coat, with his belly tucked up to his back, and ſeems as if he was wrenched in the loins. If the above complaint ſeems dangerous, and there is an appearance of an inflammation: then bleed often in ſmall quantities, and repeat Emollient Clyſters; and obſerve to give the Mallows and Parſley Water for his common drinking during all his illneſs. Alſo make uſe of the following balls.

For GRAVEL in the KIDNEYS.

Take Bracken's Cordial Ball two pounds, ſee page 28, Balſam of Sulphur drawn with Oil of Turpentine three ounces,

Of HURTS in the KIDNEYS.

Barbadoes Tar two ounces, Venice Turpentine two ounces, Nitre Salts three ounces, Spermaceti two ounces, Castile Soap two ounces, Honey four ounces, and Garlic three ounces; Tincture of Cantharides one ounce, made up into a ball with Juniper Berries in powder, for use. Give of the above, a moderate sized ball every other day; give more or less, according as they operate, and observe in the above case, to give the following decoction for his common drinking during all his illness: that is, boil Marsh Mallows, and Parsley-roots or Herbs in all his Water, that he has for his common drinking, during the whole time of his complaint.

A Valuable CLEANSER of the KIDNEYS.

Take Tincture of Cantharides one tea-spoonful, Camphire one dram, dissolved in a little Spirits of Wine, Nitre Salts and Castile Soap, of each one ounce, and Honey one ounce, made up into a ball with Diapente for one dose: to be given every fourth day, or according as they operate, repeat of the above balls, three or four doses.

A Stimulating Poultice for an ULCER in the KIDNEYS.

Take Oil of Turpentine and Spirits of Wine, of each two ounces, Garlic, Horse-radish, and Mustard-seed of each one ounce, Camphire one ounce, and Soft Soap four ounces, make a Poultice thereof cold, all together: then spread it moderate thick upon the loin part, and cover it up with a blanket.— The above may be repeated every other day, or as symptoms may require the use of it.

To Stop BLOOD from an ULCER in the KIDNEYS.

Take Bole Armoniac two ounces, Japan Earth one ounce, and Sweet Milk two quarts, mixed and made warm together

and

and given as a drink for one dofe. The above to be repeated every day for ten days together.

To Stop BLOOD from an ULCER in the KIDNEYS.

Take Bole Armoniac one ounce, Japan Earth one ounce, Roch Allum two drams, and Elixir of Vitriol one dram, made up into a ball with Sirup of Marſh Mallows for one dofe. Give one of the above balls every morning for eight mornings together. Give all the above medicines for an Ulcer in the Kidneys, according as they operate; obferve that all the medicines for an Ulcer in the Kidneys go off ſharp by urine: then ſtrictly obferving to give every dofe time to operate, before another is repeated.

Section, 19.

Of a DIABETES or Overflowing of the URINE, commonly called the JAW-PISS.

THE ſymptoms of the above diforder are, a Horfe will piſs often, and much at a time, in ſo much, that the ſtable will be overflowed in a morning; he will ſhrink in his fleſh, and his eyes ſhrunk in his head, and have a ſtaring coat, and crave much for Water; in the firſt place, let all the Water he has for his common drinking, be well boiled, with a ſufficient quantity of Bean Flour, during the whole time of his illneſs.

For a DIABETES.

Take four or ſix unſlacked Lime Stones; put them into a ſtable pail; then fill the pail up with Water, and ſtir it about

with

with a stick, next morning when the Water is clear; let the Horse have two quarts of the above Water mixed with his common Water, three times a-day; and to be repeated as symptoms may require the use of it.

A BALL for a DIABETES.

Take Sirup of Marsh Mallows one ounce, Lucatellus Balsam one ounce, Spermaceti half an ounce, Diascordium half an ounce, Bole Armoniac one ounce, made up into two balls with Diapente for one dose: if the above case should prove obstinate, the above balls are to be continued once a-day for eight or ten days together, or as symptoms may require the use of them.

A DRINK for a DIABETES.

Take Isinglass one ounce and a half chopped small, Gum Arabic one ounce bruised, then boil the above in two quarts of Sweet Milk until the whole are dissolved together; give the above for one dose. The above to be repeated once a-day for six days together; and at the same time give moderate exercise all the time in the above disorder, if possible he can bear exercise, for gentle walking exercise will forward the cure much.

Section, 20.

Of the STRANGLES and DISTEMPER.

ALL young Horses and Colts are subject to the Strangles: the symptoms of this disorder are at the first stage, a Colt will seem to be dull and heavy in his eyes, with a staring coat, and will single by himself to some remote part of the pasture, alone,

Of the STRANGLES.

alone, and will not follow his companions; and foon will appear to fwell about his jaws and glands; and at fome other times will break out in blotches all over as a rafh, the fame appearance all Horfes have, that are feized with the Diftemper that has raged fo long among Horfes in this kingdom. The above Diftemper firft appeared in this kingdom, to the beft of my memory, in the year one thoufand feven hundred and fifty, or fifty-one at furtheft, and ftill continues among Horfes to this prefent time: this Diftemper in general contracts the mufcles and deprives them of true actions. Both of the above diforders are to be treated much alike, and not to tamper with neither much in the medicine way. In the firft ftage of either of the above diforders, immediately bleed plentifully; but particularly obferving not to bleed when the diforder is thoroughly grafted in the blood, for if they are bled in the height of the diforder it is certain death. Then obferve to give moift food, fuch as fcalded Bran and Oats, or boiled Barley or the like, but if coftive which generally is the cafe, give fcalded Rye inftead of Oats with the Bran, and obferve to fupply them with Watergruel as often as you can: then obferve the following directions.

An OINTMENT for the STRANGLES.

Take two large double handfuls of the Flowers of Foxglove bruifed in a mortar, then add Hogs-lard fix pounds, and boil them all together: let the Ointment ftew over a flow fire for one hour; then ftrain it off for ufe. Rub the fwellings or tumors with the above Ointment once a-day; it will mollify the tumor or abfcefs and bring it to a head: then when quite ripe, cut the abfcefs open, and heal them with the digeftive Green Ointment for wounds in general, fee page 81. But if the above cafe fhould prove an inward fore throat, and not the leaft appearance of an abfcefs or fwelling to form matter outwardly, make ufe as follows. Take of the above Ointment three ounces, Spirits of Wine and Camphire one ounce, and Spirits of Hartfhorn four drams, mixed together cold, rub the valve and glands well with the above and keep the part warm with a cap-hood, and fluff the hood full in the infide with hot horfe-muck, out of a horfe-mixen, once a-day.

A WASH to Deftroy FUNGOUS or PROUD FLESH in the above Wound if occafion be.

Take one quart of ftrong Lime Water, diffolve therein three drams of Sublimate Mercury, and keep it in a bottle for ufe: wafh the wound with the above Fungous Water before every dreffing with the digeftive Green Ointment; and if the kernels or tumors underneath the jaws and glands ftill continue hard and gummy, make ufe of the Mercurial Quickfilver Ointment, fee page 68, and rub it well in: repeat the fame for a fortnight once every day, and it will wafte the gummy parts fine. But if the fever keeps high, and there is a danger of fuffocating from the inflammation; then you muft make ufe of fome foft Emollient Poultice, fuch as follows.

A Valuable POULTICE for the STRANGLES.

Take a large double handful of Wool, draw and open it well with your hands, then form it as a Wad; then put it into a frying-pan; add as much Hogs-lard as will make it mellow, then make the above hot together and apply it all round the Glands, and fet on a Cap-hood over all, to keep it warm to the part. Repeat the above once a-day, until you fee the tumor or abfcefs come to a head, then cut it open; then heal

and

Of the STRANGLES. 55

and cleanfe the wound with the digeftive Green Ointment, fee page 81, then it would be proper to give the Alterative Powders, in all the Mafhes you give in the Strangles and the Diftemper; a meat-fpoonful to be given once or twice a-day; the Alterative Powders are to be prepared as follows.

The ALTERATIVE POWDERS.

Take Liver of Antimony one pound and a half in very fine powder, Flour of Brimftone half a pound, Nitre Salts half a pound, mixed all together, then put the whole into a bladder for ufe. But if the fever fhould run high and contract the mufcles and render them fhort of action, give as follows.

Take Diapente one ounce, Cream of Tartar half an ounce, Flour of Brimftone one ounce, Nitre Salts one ounce, Liver of Antimony in very fine powder two ounces, Camphire two drams diffolved in a little Spirits of Wine, then mixed all together in a mortar and given for one dofe in a quart of Watergruel; repeat the above for three or four mornings together, if occafion may require the ufe of it, and at the fame time if coftive, give foft Emollient Clyfters, then if the running at the nofe fhould continue longer than common, make ufe as follows.

Take Rue a full handful, Guaiacum-wood two ounces, and Rufty Steel two pounds, all boiled together in four quarts of Forge Water until it confumes to two quarts; give one quart of the above Water, to which add Diapente two ounces for one dofe. Repeat this drink for ten mornings together, at the fame time if occafion be, give the nofe drink, a meat-fpoonful down each noftril every morning fafting, for ten mornings together before his exercife, fee Nofe Drink, page 36, when the

Horfe

Horse or Colt has recovered his strength and disorder, then it will be proper to give him gentle mild physic, as it will cause a Colt to thrive well after it. I recommend the Hiera Picra Spices, see page 18.

Section, 21.

Of BOTS and WORMS.

I Shall not pother the reader with this, that, and the other sort of Worms. So far as this, I have seen three different sorts of Worms in the stomach and bowels of a Horse when dead. The Bots are a short thick trunch, much like unto a large Maggot full of weapons, and appear in the spring and summer time of the year to stick to the outside of the fundament, and several of them come off that way; and there are other sorts of Worms which are called the red small Needle Worms, and the great long Stomach Worms. I have seen a Horse convulsed from the effect of Worms, to such a degree, that the poor creature soon ended in death, and when dead, the Bots were found to have eaten the stomach quite through in several places into holes; at the same time had galled the inside of the stomach quite raw. And what is proper to destroy the one, will destroy all the other sorts of Worms.

When a Horse has Worms, they will stick to the outside of the fundament, and there will appear a white matter or a milky-like dry substance on the outside of the fundament.— When a Horse has a fit from the effect of Worms, he will

stamp

Of the BOTS.

stamp his feet to his belly, and lie down and soon start up again, and will not roll on his back like a Horse in a fit of the Gripes: and at some other times he will tuck himself up all of a ruck, much like unto a cowed fighting-cock. Also, will appear at some other times different symptoms; that is, he will instantly be pierced in the stomach, as if he was suddenly seized with a violent cramp in the stomach and so-forth.

For BOTS or WORMS.

At first when you see a Horse have a fit from the effect of Worms, take a quart of blood from him; catch the blood, and add a full handful of Common Salt to the blood and give it as a drink: the above will ease him for that present time, then give as follows.

To Destroy WORMS in the following easy Method.

Take new Milk one quart, Honey half a pound; dissolve the above together. Give the above in a morning fasting, and let him fast two hours after the above drink; then give him a quart of strong Beef-brine made warm; and let him fast two hours after the Brine. Repeat the above method four mornings together. The repetition of the above will kill Worms of all kinds; then in two days after the above drinks, give Liver of Antimony in fine powder on all his Mashes, for some time together, one meat-spoonful in the course of a-day.

A PURGE to Destroy WORMS.

Take Barbadoes Aloes one ounce, Cream of Tartar half an ounce, Diapente one ounce, Salt of Tartar one dram, Calomel that has been well prepared one dram, Race Ginger one dram in powder, and Oil of Annifeeds forty drops, made up into a ball, with Sirup of Buckthorn for one dose. The above to be be repeated once a week, or as symptoms may require the use of it. Do not stir the Horse out during the time this physic is operating, but indulge him with gentle exercise between his Purges: observe to give a Horse time to brace and become quite lively before physic of the above kind is repeated.

A PURGE to Destroy WORMS.

Take Barbadoes Aloes six drams, Spermaceti one dram, Scammony two drams, Æthiops Mineral four drams, Diapente one ounce, Race Ginger powdered one dram, Salt of Tartar two drams, and Oil of Savin one dram, made up into a ball with Sirup of Buckthorn for one dose. The above to be repeated as symptoms may require the use of it, that is, once a week.

A Safe PURGE to Destroy WORMS.

Take Barbadoes Aloes one ounce, Spermaceti one dram, Jalap two drams, Diapente one ounce, Myrrh two drams, Salt of Tartar one dram, Oil of Savin one dram, made up into a ball with Sirup of Buckthorn for one dose. The above to be repeated once a week, or according as symptoms may require the use of it.

A Strong PURGE to Destroy WORMS.

Take Quicksilver, and Venice Turpentine of each half an ounce, mixed and killed together, until the Mercury disappears to the eye, then add Barbadoes Aloes one ounce, Spermaceti one dram, Race Ginger powdered one dram, Diapente one ounce, Salt of Tartar one dram, and Oil of Savin three drams, made up into a ball with Sirup of Buckthorn for one dose: keep the Horse warm and do not stir him out during this physic. The above may be repeated once a-week, or as

symptoms

symptoms may require the use of it: or you may make use of the following safe Purge.

Take the Hiera Picra Spices, see page 18, and make use of them as they are there recommended in all respects. Before you give any of the above Purges, give for two or three mornings together, the Sweet Ale Wort and Brown Sugar.

To Destroy WORMS a Safer Way.

Take Bracken's Cordial Ball one pound, see page 28,—Æthiops Mineral four ounces, Coroline or Sea-mofs two ounces, made up into a ball with Honey. Give a small ball every morning fasting, before his exercise. Repeat the above for nine mornings together.

For BOTS or WORMS.

Take Black Soap one ounce and a half, Flour of Brimstone one ounce, and one large Head of Garlic picked clean and bruised in a mortar; mix the above together; then dissolve the whole in a pint of warm Ale, then add Common Linseed Oil one pint; give the above for one dose. Give the Sweet Ale Wort and Brown Sugar before you give the above dose. The above to be repeated every fourth day: give three of the above doses.

To Destroy WORMS the following Simple Way.

Take Rue, Savin, and Bearsfoot, of each a double handful, chopped small, then for use; give a meat-spoonful of the above on every feed of Corn he has for ten or twelve days together.

Or this for the SAME.

Take the best Small-cut Tobacco, and give one ounce a-day, divide some upon one feed of Corn, and some upon another, so that he has one ounce a-day given him. The above to be repeated for a fortnight together.

Section, 22.

Of BROKEN-WINDED HORSES.

I Will not set down the particular symptoms of this incurable disorder, as it is so well known to all men that have had the least of practice among Horses; neither shall I boast or pretend to cure the above; however, Horses seldom become Broken-winded until they are full aged, that is, six or seven years old: I cannot give any reason why a Horse should fail at that age. But this, I know, that when a Horse comes to his full age, he is furnished in all his make, and becomes full in his muscles, and full grown in all his whole frame, both within and without, and for this reason the lungs have not the usual liberty to move and act, as they had when the Horse was young, and thriving, and if a pursive Horse takes the least of cold, his lungs will swell, as if his chest would not contain them, also, has great difficulty in breathing and so-forth. But however I will lay down some useful methods for to keep a Broken-winded Horse easy, and to do a deal of work with pleasure; which are as follow.

Horses that are Thick-winded ought to be bled once a fortnight or three weeks at furthest: observe at the same time to sprinkle all his Hay with Spring Water, and to wet all his Corn with old Lant; also, repeated Rowels are of great service to

Of BROKEN-WINDED HORSES.

to aſſiſt and relieve Thick-winded Horſes, that is, to keep one conſtantly in, it matters not where; and by theſe means you may keep a purſive Horſe eaſy; but if the complaint ſhould become more troubleſome, make uſe as follows.

To prevent a HORSE being BROKEN-WINDED, if given in Time.

Take two moderate ſized Heads of Garlic picked clean, bruiſe them in a mortar, and boil them in a quart of Sweet Skim Milk, with four ounces of Honey, then add Anniſeeds in powder two ounces, then give the whole as a drink. Give the above every morning for a fortnight together; walk him out after each doſe for an hour, keep warm and give warm Water and Maſhes during the time you give the drinks.

The MERCURIAL PURGE for a BROKEN-WINDED HORSE.

Take Calomel that has been well prepared from one dram to two, Bracken's Cordial Ball one ounce, ſee page 28, and Diapente one ounce, mixed together and made up into a ball with Honey. Let this ball be given in a morning, and let the Horſe faſt three hours before the ball, and three hours after it. Keep him warm and do not ſtir him out during this method, and give warm Water, and ſcalded or dry Bran, and Sweet Hay, and no Corn. The next morning give the following Purge.

Take the beſt Barbadoes Aloes one ounce, Jalap one dram, Spermaceti one dram, Salt of Tartar one dram, Race Ginger powdered one dram, Oil of Anniſeeds thirty drops, and Diapente one ounce, made up into a ball with Sirup of Buckthorn for one dose, let the above method be repeated three times; but be sure you give the Horse time to recover between each dose, before the above is repeated. Then repeat the Mercurial Ball and the Purge as above directed in all respects; and give the Gum Arabic Water between his doses, mixed with all his common Water, that is, one ounce a-day diffolved in a pint of hot Water and mixed with his common Water.

A MOLLIFYING DRINK.

To be given between the above Purges for four mornings together if occasion requires the use of it.

Take Hyssop, Horchound and Coltsfoot, of each a single handful, and Linseed half a pint, boil the whole in a quart of Water; then cover it up for all night. In the morning add to the above, Annifeeds and Liquorice powder of each one ounce and Saffron one dram, then sweeten the above with Treacle for one dose. The above is very healing and comfortable.

After you have made use of the above method, and the Mercurial Purges are operated, give the following ball every morning.

Take Gum Ammoniacum, Gum Galbanum and Assafœtida, of each two ounces, Garlic four ounces, Cinnabar of Antimony six ounces, Saffron half an ounce, Oxymel of Squills three ounces, and Elecampane one pound, made up into a ball with Honey. Give of the above a small ball for one dose, every morning for a fortnight together.

A PURGE for THICK-WINDED HORSES.

Take of the best Barbadoes Aloes one ounce, Gum Myrrh, Gum Galbanum and Gum Ammoniacum, of each two drams, Saffron

Of BROKEN-WINDED HORSES.

Saffron one dram, Salt of Tartar one dram, Diapente one ounce, Oil of Annifeeds thirty drops, the Powers of Amber a tea-fpoonful, made up into a ball with Sirup of Buckthorn for one dofe. They that do not venture to give the Mercurial Phyfic, may depend that this is a fafe Purge for the purpofe. The above to be repeated once a week, or as the Horfe requires the ufe of it.

To Cleanfe and Clear a Foul Purfive STOMACH.

The following is proper to be given after a Horfe is taken up from Grafs.

Take the Roots of Polypody of the Oak, a fmall handful; cleanfe them, and bruife them in a mortar; then add to the Roots, half an ounce of Oil of Spikenard, mix them together in a mortar; then wrap the Roots and Oil up in a linen cloth, and tie them to the middle part of a fnaffle-bit; then in the morning fafting, put the fame bridle-bit in the Horfe's mouth and ride him gently for an hour; then bring him in and give him two hornfuls of White Wine and Honey made hot together; then let him faft for an hour; then give him a warm Mafh: then his Hay. Obferve to give in the above cafe warm Water during the whole time. The next morning repeat the fame, as above directed, and fo continue for twelve mornings together, the fame Roots and Oil will ferve for the whole time. The above method will caufe the Horfe to flime and flaver much: the above will cleanfe a foul purfive Stomach, or an old cough; efpecially if the following method is made ufe of after.

Take Liver of Antimony two pounds in very grofs lumps, or powder; put the whole into a two-gallon earthen bottle; then

then fill the bottle up with Old Lant, and let it stand for a week, but observe to shake the bottle every day; then clear off a quart bottleful for use, and wet all his Corn with the above Lant, and as you take one quart out of the earthen bottle, put one quart of fresh Lant into the same bottle again. The Antimony will serve you for ever, and will answer the same purpose. Or you may instead of the above Antimony and Lant Decoction, make use of the Squills Drink for a Wheezing in the Stomach, see page 36, and observe the directions there given in all respects.

For a BROKEN-WINDED HORSE.

First bleed, then give two ounces of Quickfilver; one ounce to be given down each nostril in a morning fasting, and let him fast four hours after each dose. The above to be repeated for eight mornings together.

Continue bleeding every week; at the same time indulge him with Mashes and warm Water, and let him be in a loose warm Stable during the whole time.

The above was communicated to me by a worthy Gentleman, a friend of mine, who says it never failed a cure; and since then I have found it to answer well.

As the following ADVERTISEMENT,

In the public paper, was communicated to the public in general, and I having the opportunity to see it, I then thought it a pack of stuff; but since then, I was informed by a worthy Gentleman, a friend of mine, who had made a trial of the Receipt, and found it to answer a cure on two of his own Horses. I therefore thought it my duty to give it a place here.

The

Of BROKEN-WINDED HORSES.

The following is a true copy of the original Advertisement. A cheap and easy cure for a Broken-winded Horse.—A Broken-winded Horse had been kept in a field where there was no Water, except in the bottom of an old lime kiln, and had recovered his wind, the owner of him ordered a stable shovelful of quick-lime to be renewed every five or six days, and the Water to be poured off, and a bucketful of it to be given every day to a Broken-winded Coach-horse, about eighteen years old, which had almost a constant cough: the Horse was watered with Water thus prepared for about five weeks, and kept in a stable. He is now perfectly recovered in his wind, and free from a cough; by applying the above remedy.

To keep a BROKEN-WINDED HORSE easy for one Day.

The night before and the morning you mean to use him, give him the following drink.

Take a sheet of the best Writing Paper, and a quart of Sweet Milk, and pound them together in a mortar to a pulp or chyle, then for use. Give a quart of the above the night before, and the same in the morning you mean to use him; keep him empty from Water. The above will keep him easy and free for that Day's work.

Observe to bleed plentifully a week before the time you mean to give him the above. But if any Horse should be completely Broken-winded, the only method to give him ease will be to employ a man of practice, to make him an artificial or false fundament, and by the use of that will ease him much and enable him to do business with ease and pleasure.

Section, 23.

Of SURFEITS in General.

THE symptoms of a Surfeit are, a Horse will have a foul staring coat, and seem to be open, and full of scales and scurf, and some times with small lumps and blotches all over his body, and itches much with a wet humor attending the parts; at some other times will fly to the Withers, and the violent itching and heat, will cause the Horse to rub, and scrub so much as to bring on a great inflammation, and will cause the part to be ulcerated, and will become dangerous, and some times will fall down into his limbs, and if not care taken, will soon become a Farcy, or a moving Lameness, first in one part and then in another.

The cause of this disorder at first, is generally, when a Horse has been hot and sweated much, and cooled too sudden, by some unthinking rider that has tied a Horse to a hedge when hot, and by so doing has stagnated the Pores of the Skin. At other times by the ill effect of mouldy-flooded Hay, or bad stinking Corn, or by the ill effect of a damp stable, especially when a Horse has been well used with care at his own stable at home.

For a SURFEIT.

In the first place bleed often in small quantities, then give the following Purge.

Take

Of SURFEITS. 67

Take Barbadoes Aloes one ounce, Diapente half an ounce, Cream of Tartar half an ounce, Jalap one dram, Liver of Antimony one ounce in fine powder, Salt of Prunella half an ounce, Gum Myrrh one dram, made up into a ball with Sirup of Buckthorn for one dose. The above to be repeated once a week; give three of the above Purges.

A DRINK to be given after the above Purges has operated, that is, in three Days after.

Take Oil of Anniseeds one ounce, Diapente, Turmeric, Liquorice Powder and Flour of Brimstone, of each one ounce, Liver of Antimony in very fine powder six ounces; all mixed together in a mortar, then divided for two drinks and given in a quart of warm Ale. The above to be repeated every other morning; give four of the above drinks. If a Surfeit should prove obstinate, give a course of the following balls.

Take Cinnabar of Antimony, Gum Guaiacum and Castile Soap, of each half a pound, Flour of Brimstone one pound, and Camphire one ounce and a half, made up into a ball with Honey, give a small ball of the above every morning fasting, for ten or twelve mornings together. If the above balls should work much by urine, then observe to give one every other morning, or according as they operate. This method properly observed will cure most Surfeits whatever.

In some INVETERATE SURFEITS,

That have much breakings out, as dry or wet blotches all over the body and cause much itching; I would advise to dress the Horse all over with the slender Mercurial Ointment, then rub it on well in the sun or by a fire; keep the Horse warm after, for six or eight days, as this Ointment will be apt to to caufe him to purge. As I have not mentioned how to make the Mercurial Ointment, its prepared as follows.

The MERCURIAL OINTMENT.

Take Oil of Turpentine and Venice Turpentine of each two ounces, Quickfilver four ounces; kill the above well together in a mortar until the Mercury difappears to the eye; then add two pounds of rendered Hogs-lard, mix them all together until cold; then for ufe. If I meant the above to be made weaker, I added more Hogs-lard to it. But in fome fharp humors in the fkin, fimilar to the above cafe, I recommend to make ufe of the Alterative Powders, fee page 55, and to the fame quantity there directed, add thereunto Æthiops Mineral four ounces, mix the whole well together. And obferve the fame directions as is there given in all refpects. The above if repeated has a great fhare in checking moft fharp humors, Efpecially if given after a hard day's work, on a good Mafh of Bran and Oats.

Section, 24.

Of FARCIES in General.

THE Farcy is well known to all men that have had the leaft of practice among Horfes, its one of the filthieft diforders that happens to a Horfe: the fymptoms are a rafh humor that fpreads all over the whole body, but at fome other times it might fix in one leg, or about the neck and throat; then foon will become in hard lumps, and foon break out into holes and ulcers, and there will appear to run out of the

Of the FARCY.

the ulcers a bad bloody matter, and will move from one part to another, and the wounds will appear much like unto a hen's fundament, when it opens and shuts with the discharge of excrement; and at other times will run all over the whole body with broad ulcers of the above kind; if so, it will be very catching to other Horses and the like.

The Water Farcy is a swelling that settles all along the under part of the Belly, insomuch that it will appear to be four inches deep, much like unto a large cushion full of watery humor or Serum Water.

For the FARCY.

At the first stage of this distemper bleed plentifully, then rub the part with the following mixture. Take Oil of Turpentine six ounces, and put it in a large quart bottle, then add Oil of Vitriol two ounces, drop the Oil of Vitriol into the Oil of Turpentine by a little at a time until the whole is mixed together; then for use. Rub the part well with the above mixture. This mixture with the help of a few drinks will cure any fresh Farcy whatever. Observe to rub the part with the above mixture twice only, that is once every other day and no more.

To Destroy the FARCY BUDS that Spreads all over the whole Body.

Take Realgar and Sublimate of each one ounce, Yellow Arsenic and Euphorbium of each half an ounce; make all the above in fine powder, then add Oil of Bays with Quicksilver four ounces; then mix the whole cold together into an Ointment; then for use. When used cut the Buds across with a Lancet, then dip a small pledget of Tow with the above Oin-

ment and apply it into the Buds, and let it remain in.—
The above application will core the Buds out, and will cause
a cure without any other application whatever.

For a FARCY that Flies all over the whole Body.

Take Spirits of Wine four ounces, Oil of Vitriol and Oil of
Turpentine of each two ounces, and Old Strong Beer one
pint, mixed all together for use: then rub the part well with
the above mixture, and it will add much to the cure of the
Farcy. Farcies of all kinds ought to be treated outwardly as
well as inwardly. Or you may make use of the following,
which is much stronger.

A Strong MIXTURE for the FARCY.

Take Linseed Oil half a pint, Oil of Turpentine and Oil of
Petre of each two ounces, Tincture of Euphorbium one ounce,
Tincture of Hellebore two ounces, the Strong Mercurial Ointment three ounces, see page 68, Oil of Origanum and Double
Aquafortis of each one ounce, and Barbadoes Tar three
ounces, all mixed together for use. Rub the parts well with
the above mixture twice only, that is, once every other day
and no more.

If the Buds appear after the use of any of the above mixture, to look thin about the edges and seem to run a good
matter, it is a symptom of a speedy cure.

A DRINK for the FARCY or GREASE.

First bleed plentifully, then take Gentian one ounce, Birthwort two ounces, and Sarsaparilla one ounce, all sliced thin,
then infuse the above in three pints of Lime Water for twenty-four hours, then strain it off, and give the Decoction as a drink;

Of the FARCY.

drink; then take the same roots and steep them for twenty-four hours again, in three pints of Old Lant, then give the Lant as a Drink the third day; let the Horse fast three hours before each drink, and four hours after each drink. If the above Drinks should not perfect a cure; make use of the following balls.

A BALL for the FARCY.

Take Quicksilver and Venice Turpentine of each one ounce; kill the above well together in a mortar, until the Mercury disappears to the eye, then add Venice Treacle one ounce, Camphire one dram and a half dissolved in a little Spirits of Wine, and Tincture of Cantharides one tea-spoonful, made up into two balls with Diapente for one dose. Give one of the above doses every fifth day, fasting four hours before each dose, and four hours after each dose. Observe to give warm Water and Mashes; and make use of a loose stable. Five of the above doses is sufficient for a cure.

The PRECIPITATE BALL for the FARCY.

Take Red Precipitate one dram and a half, finely levigated, and Venice Treacle, one ounce and a half mixed together and made up into a ball with Diapente for one dose; give four of the above balls, one every fourth day, and use the same precaution with this ball, as with the former ball in all respects.

A DRINK for the FARCY.

First bleed plentifully; then take Rue and Hogs-lard of each a like quantity, pounded together in a mortar, and stop each ear up with the above; then tie the ears up with a list. Then take a double handful of Common Mallows bruised in a mortar, and mixed with a quart of Old Lant; then strain it off, and

and give the decoction for one drink, give one of the above drinks every other morning. Repeat five of the above drinks.

A STRONG DRINK for an INVETERATE FARCY.

Take Rue, Burdock, Salendine, Wormwood, Ashes of Green Broom, Hemlock, and Dwarf-elder, of each a full double handful; boil the above in six quarts of Old Lant until it consumes to four quarts; then strain the liquor off for use. Then add to one quart of the above decoction, Lapis Calaminaris, Brown Tartar, Gentian, and Birthwort, of each half an ounce. Give the above for one drink, every other day. Repeat four of the above drinks according to the above directions, and at the same time let the Horse have the Lime Water for his common drinking, during all the time of the cure.

A STRONG PLAISTER for the FARCY, that has Settled in one or more Legs, which appears full of ulcerated Buds.

Take Venice Turpentine one pound, Quicksilver eight ounces, Oil of Turpentine two ounces; kill the above well together in a mortar until the Mercury disappears; then add to the above the Strong Quicksilver Ointment three ounces, and Burgundy Pitch one pound. Then mix the whole together for use; when used apply a Plaister of the above spread upon Tow to the part, and bind it on with a Flannel Roller, and repeat it again in four or five days to come; and let the Animal be kept in a dry loose stable all the time. The repetition of the above Plaister will destroy the Buds and cause a cure.

For the WATER FARCY.

First of all fleam the swelling that is underneath the belly, with a hot fleam, in fifteen or twenty places, so that the

Of the FARCY.

watery humor or Serum Water may run off; then rub the part well with equal parts of Strong Beer and Oil of Turpentine shook well together in a bottle, then for use. Then immediately foment the part with Old Lant and Wood Ashes well boiled together; then give the following Drinks for four or five mornings together, or every other morning, or according as you see occasion require the use of them.

If the above application should fail, make two, three, or four Incisions in the Swelling under the Belly, with a hot Iron Chisel an inch and a half wide quite through the skin and membrane, then flay each orifice the whole length of your finger all round; then fill each orifice with Tow and Oil of Turpentine, and treat the orifices as a rowel.

A DRINK for the WATER FARCY.

Take a quart of Old Lant and boil therein two pounds of Rusty Steel or Iron; then strain it off, and add to the decoction, Ashes of Green Broom two ounces, and Diapente one ounce, mixed together for one drink. Then give the following drink if occasion require the use of it. Take one quart of Ale, and boil therein a full handful of Rue and the same quantity of Hemlock, then add to the above decoction, Diapente one ounce, Liver of Antimony in fine powder two ounces; when mixed all together, add Tincture of Steel one dram; then given for one drink; repeat the above drink one every other day. Give three of the above drinks.

Section, 25.

########

Of a HORSE or COW that has Licked up some Venomous Animal, or is Over-gorged with Clover or Turnips, or any such luscious Food.

THE symptoms are, a Horse or Cow will seem to be swelled much, as if they would burst. First bleed plentifully, then give as follows.

Take Castile Soap two ounces, Sirup of Marsh Mallows three ounces mixed together in a mortar, then dissolved in a pint of warm Ale for one dose: give the above as soon as you can, then stir the Horse gently about, and it will cause him to purge easy, and piss much. If the above doth not succeed in two hours time, give the following drink.

Take Lisbon Wine one pint, Camphire two drams and a half dissolved in a little Spirits of Wine, Oil of Juniper two drams, the Powers of Amber two drams and Sirup of Marsh Mallows four ounces, mixed together for one drink, and given in a pint of warm Ale: then stir the Horse about very gently. The above will cause him to piss and empty himself plentifully. At the same time give the Mallows and Parsley Water, in the above case, for his common drinking, during his whole complaint, or as long as symptoms may require the use of it. That is, to boil plenty of Marsh Mallows and and Parsley in his common Water for the whole time, of his illness. And if the above case should prove obstinate, and there should be an appearance of an inflammation in the bowels;

Of the GLANDERS.

bowels; then make ufe of the following Clyfter. Take Sena two ounces and boil it in two quarts of foft Water for half an hour; then ftrain it off, and add to the decoction, Common Treacle one pound and Sweet Oil half a pint; then for ufe. The above Clyfter to be repeated three times a-day, or as occafion may require the ufe of it. In the recovery of the above it would be very proper to give a gentle eafy purge or two; as fo, make ufe of the following.

Take the Hiera Picra Spices, fee page 18, from feven to ten drams, or one ounce and a half might be given or as the habit or ftrength of the Horfe's body requires it: made up into a ball with Sirup of Buckthorn, for one dofe. The above will purge him mild and eafy. Obferve to ufe the fame precautions with the above, as you would with other purging phyfic in all refpects.

Section 26.

Of GLANDERED HORSES.

THE fymptoms of this foul and incurable diftemper, are at the firft ftage, a Horfe will feem to run at the nofe a thin waterifh humor, and at the fame time the Kernels underneath and between the Jaws or Glands will feem to knot and fwell; then foon will appear to run at the nofe a yellow or green ftinking matter, and fome other times will difcharge a black matter; and if the cafe fhould prove fo, all hope of a cure is over: and I do advife the owner to accompany no other Horfe with this. If he runs a black matter at the nofe,

that

that is a sure sign that the grisly honey-comb bones within the head are rotting and decaying daily, so there is no hope of a cure; if so, this distemper oft proceeds from a broken constitution, or by an ill-cured distemper, such as Fevers, Farcies, Surfeits, or the like; I always found it a good twenty to one against a cure. Although M. La-fosse, and several other authors have given their directions and methods of trepanning, yet I have not seen nor heard of any Horse that was trepanned, but what ended in death: however, I will agree with M. La-fosse's judgment, in pointing out the true seat of the above disorder, as I was an eye-witness to several Horses in this distemper, when dead I have dissected the heads of them, and found the whole seat of the disorder to be in the grisly bones of the nostrils and head adjoining to the brain, and found all that part quite rotten, and full of matter much of the cancerous kind; therefore there is no hope of a cure of such. But however I will give you the following directions. That is, if you have to do with the above disorder it must be in the first stage of it.

First bleed, and keep warm; then make use of Scalded Bran with a very little Oats for Mashes, with warm Water, and a little Sweet Hay, and no other kind of food, indulging him with gentle exercise all the while. Then fumigate his head three times a-day with hot Mashes, then immediately after the fumigating or stimulating with the said Mashes; pour down each nostril a very small hornful of the following decoction.

Take a full double handful of Rosemary, and boil it in four quarts of Forge Water; then add Honey of Roses half a pound and Sugar of Lead two ounces, boil the whole together, then

strain

Of the GLANDERS.

ſtrain it off for uſe. After you have made uſe of the above, make uſe of the following Spirituous Mixture, at the ſame time the above Roſemary Decoction is made uſe of.

Take Spirits of Wine very ſtrongly camphorated two ounces, Spirits of Hartſhorn one ounce, Sweet Oil ſix ounces, all mixed together. Rub the Valves and Glands from ear to ear with the above once a-day, and put a Cap-hood on his Head, and ſtuff the Hood within all round up to the Glands and Ears, with hot Horſe-muck out of a Horſe-dunghill, and repeat the ſame once a-day, which will forward the cure much, then make uſe of the following Ball.

A BALL for the GLANDERS.

Take Matthew's Pill four drams, ſee page 35, and Bracken's Cordial Ball two ounces, ſee page 28, mix the above together for one doſe: give one of the above balls every morning faſting, for ten days together, indulging him with gentle exerciſe all the time; and after the uſe of the above ball, make uſe of the following drink.

The NOSE DRINK in the GLANDERS,

Take White Wine Vinegar, and White Wine of each half a pint; fine Tobacco, Burnt Allum, and Roſemary in powder of each one ounce, Saffron half an ounce all in fine powder, and Honey of Roſes two ounces, all ſimmered together, then ſtrained and bottled for uſe; when the above drink is cold, add Balſam Capivy one ounce, and the Yolk of an Egg, then mix the Balſam and the Egg well together, and add it to the above, and ſhake the whole well together, then for uſe: give of the above two meat-ſpoonfuls down each noſtril in a morning faſting, before his exerciſe for a fortnight together. After you have made use of the above, you may proceed as follows. Take Flour of Brimstone and Fresh Butter of each one ounce, and Sugar of Lead two drams, mix the above together for use; then take two large Goose-quills, dip and rub the feathery ends of the quills in the above mixture, then put one of the quills up each nostril, then tie a piece of packthread to the hard end of each quill, and tie the packthread over the Horse's poll as a headstal of a bridle; then ride him for one hour every day, with the feathers anointed as above directed. Keep him warm during the whole time. The above method will cleanse his head much, and free the Glands from slimy snot and filthiness; should the Kernels underneath and about the Glands still continue hard and gummy, rub the part well twice a-day with the strong Mercurial Ointment, which will if repeated waste the part fine.

Section, 27.

Of a HORSE BURNT by a MARE.

THE symptoms of the above are as follow, the Horse's penis and testicles will swell, and the thin membrane of the yard or penis will seem to be galled in specks and blotches, and for the most part will appear to hang out of the scrotum or sheath, with a constant running or gleet at the end of the penis. First bleed moderately, and repeat bleeding as symptoms require; at the same time foment the penis and testicles with any mild fomentation of herbs, boiled in Skim-milk and Water, three times a-day; then after each fomenting, give the yard a
wash

Of a HORSE BURNT by a MARE.

wash with the following mixture. Take a quart bottleful of Spring Water, then add Sublimate Mercury two drams to the Water, then for use. Then immediately after the above wash, make use of the following Ointment.

Take Hemlock, Primrose-leaves, and Allheal of each a double handful; bruise the above in a mortar, and boil them in two pounds of Hogs-lard; then strained off for use. Liquor the penis with the above Ointment after every dressing with the former Wash or Water, and observe to give Nitre Salts in all his common Water, that is, one ounce a-day; then in four days time make use of the following Purge.

Take Sena one ounce, boil it in three half pints of Water, then strain it off, and add Glauber's Salts two ounces, Cream of Tartar two ounces, Jalap one dram, Common Treacle half a pint, Oil of Annifeeds half an ounce, and Sweet Oil four ounces, make the above warm together for one dose. Repeat the above Purge as you see occasion require the use of it, that is, once every four or five days.

To take a MARE off her PRIDE or HORSING.

Take the Herb Tansy, a double handful chopped small, put the whole into a Feed of Corn and give it her to eat; and it will take her off her Pride in one day and a night. As the above is worth notice I gave it a place here, as I could not so well place it in any of the other Sections.

To make a MARE STAND to a HORSE.

First observe the Mare, to be half gone on her pride, if possible you can guess it so to be; then let the Horse cover her four or five times in the space of one day, and the last time she is covered, open the neck-vein before the Horse gets
on

and when he is on and in action, let the Mare bleed plentifully; then immediately after give the following Drink. Take Skim-milk one quart and Common Allum one ounce; boil the above together, then ſtrain it off, and add to the Whey one ounce of Oriental Bole, then mixed together and given for one drink. Then make uſe of a looſe private Stable, for a week at leaſt; then to graſs where there are no Horſes to teaſe her.

Section, 28.

Of the ANTICOR.

THE above diſorder is common to Horſes in parts abroad, but ſeldom here in England. I have ſeen and cured in my time, ſeveral of the ſame. The ſymptoms of the above diſorder are thoſe of a ſlow fever, and commonly are coſtive in their bodies: if ſo, you muſt give ſoft mild Clyſters, and cooling ſoft Food with Nitre Salts mixed with all their common Water. Then ſoon will appear at the point of the ſhoulder adjoining to the neck-vein, or on the breaſt part, a large impoſthume tumor, which will appear to be very hard and bony, and will be apt to break inward, if not well encouraged with hot Poultices; and obſerve to rub the part well with Hogs-lard, at all times, before you put the Poultice on; then as ſoon as you find the Anticor to be ſomewhat ſoft, you muſt open the part, which will be very deep to get at, obſerve to open it well downwards in order for a drain to diſcharge the matter off, and there you will find a great quantity of matter of the chalkſtone kind to come out. Then waſh the wound

wound withinſide, with equal parts of Oil of Turpentine, and Tincture of Myrrh with Aloes, mixed together in a bottle for uſe. Then treat the wound in all reſpects as a green wound or ulcer, as I have mentioned in the following Section. Then in the latter part or the recovery of the above diſorder, it would be very proper to give two or three doſes of mild purging phyſic.

Section, 29.

Of WOUNDS in General

IN all Freſh Wounds from a ſtake, or a cut by a weapon, in the firſt place, if a vein or artery ſhould be cut, and there ſhould much blood ſeem to appear, care muſt be taken to ſtitch or tie the vein or artery up, and obſerve to cloſe the edges of the wound together. On the other hand if the rind or rim of the belly ſhould be broken or burſt, and the bowels or gut ſhould come down, care muſt be taken to put the bowels up properly, and obſerve to ſtitch the rind up, and to apply proper pledgets and cloſe bandages to the part, and obſerve not to open the wound but as ſeldom as you can; and always dip the pledgets that you lay next the wound in Spirits of Wine; then apply as follows. To all green wounds; firſt I ſay, to ſtop the blood, then proceed according to the following directions.

To ſtop Internal BLEEDING at the Noſe and Stomach.

Take the Juice of Green Nettles one quart, and if the blood comes from the Noſe, pour down each noſtril four or five meat-spoonfuls of the above Nettle Juice; and if from the Stomach, give two or three small hornfuls of the above Juice. The Nettles are to be pounded in a mortar and the Juice prest well out for the above use.

To stop BLOOD in any Part.

Take Tincture of Martis one tea-spoonful, and one meat-spoonful of Spring Water; mixed stronger or weaker according to the symptoms; syringing the above up the nostrils if the hemorrhage is there; or dip a strong pledget of Tow in the above mixture for any other part whatever.

Also to stop BLOOD from a Wound.

Take the Puff-ball or Mushroom that grows upon old pasture Lands, apply the dry Pulp thick on any wound that bleeds, and tie it up with a strong pledget of Tow with proper bandages, and let it remain on for one day; then make use of some of the digestive Ointments.

A MIXTURE to Wash GREEN WOUNDS.

I would advise that all Green Wounds should be at first washed with the following Mixture. Take Tincture of Myrrh with Aloes, and Oil of Turpentine of each two ounces, mixed together in a bottle for use. Wash or dab all Green Wounds at first, with the above Mixture, and it will forward a digestion; and at the same time make use of any of the following Digestives and Cleansing Ointments.

The Digestive GREEN OINTMENT.

Take White Rosin, Bees-wax, and Honey, of each four ounces, Venice Turpentine six ounces, and Hogs-lard one pound and a half; melt the whole together over a slow fire; then

then add to the above, Verdigreafe in fine powder two ounces; then boil all together for two minutes and no longer, then take it off the fire, and add Oil of Turpentine two ounces, ftirring all together until quite cold: then for ufe.

The YELLOW BASILICON.

Take Bees-wax and White Rofin of each half a pound, Hogs-lard one pound, and Venice Turpentine two ounces, all melted together over a flow fire: then ftirred until quite cold, then for ufe.

A HEALING CLEANSING OINTMENT.

Take Horfe Turpentine and Mutton Suet of each half a pound, White Rofin four ounces, Bees-wax two ounces, and Hogs-lard one pound, all melted together for ufe. Then, obferve at all times, after the ufe of any of the above Ointments, and the edges of the Wound fhould prove gummy or fpungy; then obferve to touch the out edges of the Wound, round the fides, with a piece of Roman Vitriol. The above method will keep the fkin thin, alfo, the cure will not appear gummy. Then obferve if an inflammation in any Wound fhould happen, to make ufe of the following fomentation.

The FOMENTATION.

Take Marfh Mallows, Common Mallows, St. John's Wort, Rofemary, Wormwood, Chickweed, Groundfel, Hemlock, Camomile, and Foxglove, of each a double handful; boil the above well in three gallons of grounds of Old Beer, and Water; then for ufe. Then foment the part well with the above, twice a-day, and obferve after each fomenting to rub the part well with Spirits of Wine and Camphire, to keep the part warm: that is, when Fomentations are made ufe of, let the

the part be always rubbed with ſtrong Spirits of Wine and Camphire, after each fomenting, or elſe the part will take cold, as Fomentations open the pores much; and if there ſhould be an appearance of a mortification, and the body ſhould be in a bad habit; then give Nitre and Bark, that is, give half an ounce of each, twice a-day in a pint of Water-gruel.

A Valuable FOMENTATION to Diſperſe a SWELLING in any Part.

Take Roman Wormwood, Common Wormwood and Bay-leaves, of each a double handful; then boil the above well in ſix quarts of Sour Lant, then foment the part well twice a-day, and make uſe of Spirits of Wine and Camphire after each Fomentation.

To Deſtroy FUNGOUS or PROUD FLESH.

Take Yellow Baſilicon ſix ounces, and Red Precipitate one ounce, mixed together for uſe. Dreſs all Green Wounds, with the above mixture, that grow up too quick, and ſeem to appear ſpungy.

To Make FRIARS BALSAM.

Take Gum Benjamin three ounces, Balſam of Tolu two ounces, Gum Storax two ounces, Succotrine Aloes one ounce, and a half, Gum Guaiacum two ounces, Frankincenſe two ounces, Gum Myrrh one ounce, Rectified Spirits of Wine two quarts, Brandy one quart; bruiſe the Gums and digeſt the whole in a large earthen bottle in a hot horſe-dunghill for ſeven days, ſhaking the bottle every day; then for uſe. The above is a good application for a ſmall cut, or a ſmall over-reach, by only dabing the part with the above.

Of WOUNDS.

To make TINCTURE of MYRRH.

Take Brandy one quart, fine Aloes, and Gum Myrrh, of each two ounces in fine powder, all mixed together: then put the above into a large quart bottle; then put the bottle in a hot horfe-midden for four days, fhaking the bottle well every day; then fit for ufe. I will advife that all Green Wounds that grow up too faft, and fill up too quick: particularly, ought not to be dreffed with any greafy application: as fo, I would advife to drefs all fuch Wounds, with dry Tow dipped in the above Tincture, and Oil of Turpentine, of each the fame quantity mixed together, in a bottle for ufe; or you may make ufe of dry Lint inftead of the above.

The HEALING and DRYING POWDER for a WOUND or ULCER.

Take Bole Ammoniac eight ounces, Roman Vitriol one ounce, Red Precipitate one ounce, all made in fine powder, and mixed together for ufe. The above is very proper to puff a Wound or Ulcer with, after you have left off the ufe of pledgets and bandages. The repetition of the above generally promotes a found cure. Alfo, the above may be applied to a Wound that is endowed with too great a gleet or moifture.

To EXFOLIATE a FOUL BONE in any WOUND or ULCER.

Take Tincture of Myrrh with Aloes one ounce, and the ftrong Tincture of Euphorbium half an ounce, mixed together in a bottle for ufe. When ufed for a foul Bone, dip a fmall pledget of Tow in the above mixture; then apply it on the Wounded Bone, then drefs the Wound up with the Mild Digeftive Red Ointment, See page 89, and continue the above dreffings,

dreffings, until the Bone is Exfoliated clear off the part, then treat the Wound as fymptoms may appear.

To Deſtroy FUNGOUS or PROUD FLESH.

Take Corrofive Sublimate two drams, diffolve the above in one quart of clear Lime Water; then bottled for ufe.—Wafh all Wounds that grow up too quick, with the above Water, then apply your other fpirituous dreffings, and proceed as neceffity requires.

For GALLED SHOULDERS, ſuch as from the Collar or Harneſs.

Take Quickfilver half a pound, Venice Turpentine four ounces, killed together; then add Hogs-lard and Goofe-greafe of each one pound, Bees-wax half a pound, Oil of Turpentine two ounces, all melted together, and ſtirred until cold. The above is very proper to drefs fcabby Sheep.

To Stop JOINT WATER.

Take Oil of Vitriol and Sublimate Mercury of each one dram, Oil of Turpentine, and Oil of Petre of each half an ounce, Spirits of Wine ſtrongly camphorated one ounce, mixed together for ufe; fyringing the above mixture into any cavity; or dip a pledget in the above mixture, and apply it to the Wound; then apply your other fpirituous dreffings on the part, and fo proceed as fymptoms may appear.

To Stop JOINT WATER.

Take Bole Ammoniac in fine powder three ounces, Roman Vitriol in fine powder one ounce, mixed together for ufe.—Puff the Wound full with the above powder, then make ufe of no greafy digeſtion: you may ufe Tincture of Myrrh and

Oil

Oil of Turpentine of each the same quantity mixed together, or the Milder Red Digestive Ointment, see page 89.

For an Obstinate JOINT WATER.

Take Oil of Turpentine and Spirits of Wine of each one ounce, Tincture of Euphorbium, Butter of Antimony, Spirits of Common Salts, Camphire, and Dragon's Blood, of each one dram, Sublimate Mercury one dram, mixed all together in a bottle for use: make use of the above sparingly with a small pledget dipped in the above mixture, and apply it to the bottom of the Wound. The above is a strong application, but is very proper for a severe Joint Water.

For a BROKEN KNEE or CUT by STUMBLING.

Take Oil of Turpentine one pint, Barbadoes Tar two ounces, and Spirits of Sal Ammoniac two ounces, mixed together for use. Rub the part well with the above, the first dressing; then only dab the Wound with a little Tow dipped in the above mixture for the dressings to come; the above will ease the pain and heal the part firm, especially if a fresh Wound; and the capsular ligament is not injured.

To Cause HAIR to GROW on any FRESH-HEALED WOUND.

Take six large Corks that have been used in Red-port bottles sliced and burnt on a fireshovel to blackness, and stirred all the while; then make the whole into powder, and add Bearsgrease two ounces, and Honey one ounce, mixed all together for use. Then anoint the part twice a-day with the above Ointment: this will cause Hair to Grow if any application will or can.

Section,

Section, 30.

Of ULCERS in General or SWELLING TUMORS.

ALL Ulcers generally proceed from a bad habit of body, and ill juices in the blood, such as move here and there, and sometimes will settle on a joint, which is the worst of parts to fix on, and in short, in various parts of the body, and if so, you must treat the inside as well as the outside for a sound cure. Ulcers will happen to a Horse after an ill-cured distemper, such as Fevers, Farcies and the like. Then I say at first, if the Ulcer or Tumor is not ripe enough to be cut open, make use of the following Ripening Poultice, and when the part is ready to be cut open, be sure to open it the whole length of the cavity, and by so doing you will forward the cure much: then proceed in all respects, as I have before mentioned in the management of Green Wounds, and continue so to do until you see the Wound come to a good digestion, and that you will in three or four dressings. Then leave off all greasy applcations; but if there should be an occasion for the Ripening Poultice, it is made as follows.

A POULTICE to RIPEN any TUMOR.

Take Mallows of both kinds a double handful, six Heads of Garlic, and as much White Lily-roots, bruise the above together in a mortar; then boil the whole in Milk and Water, and make it up into a Poultice with Oatmeal and a little Hogslard. Repeat the above Poultice as you see occasion. But at some other times, I make use of Hogs-lard alone and nothing else,

Of ULCERS.

elfe, to Ripen Tumors, but it made warm and rubbed twice a-day on the part; when ready to be cut open, cut the Ulcer the whole length of the cavity; then wafh and cleanfe the Ulcer with the following mixture. The Tincture of Myrrh with Aloes, and Oil of Turpentine of each one ounce, mixed together for ufe. Then drefs the Wound up with the following Ointment.

A Valuable POULTICE to Ripen any TUMOR or ULCER.

Take Camomile Herb and Foxglove, of each a fingle handful, chopped fmall and pounded in a mortar green together; then add Skim-milk one quart: then add three or four large Green Potatoes and grate them on a grater to a Pulp; then put the whole together into a faucepan, and boil the above to the confiftence of a Poultice; then add a little Hogs-lard to make it mellow. The repetition of the above will Ripen any Ulcer whatever.

If ufed for human Species, and repeated every day will forward any Ulcer and bring it to a head, and if repeated will perform a found cure without any other application whatever.

The Mild Digeftive RED OINTMENT.

Take Honey one pound and Verdigreafe four ounces in fine powder; boil them together until it comes to a deep Red Ointment; then ftir it until quite cold, then for ufe. The above Ointment is very proper for Ulcerated Wounds.

The Strong RED OINTMENT.

Take Burnt Allum and Borax, and Verdigreafe and White Copperas, of each one ounce, made into fine powder, and Honey two pounds; boil the whole together until it comes to a deep a deep Red Ointment, when it is almoſt cold add Aquafortis half an ounce; then ſtir the Ointment until it is quite cold, then for uſe. The above two Ointments are proper for Ulcerated Wounds, and might be made uſe of inſtead of any of the greaſy Digeſtive Ointments.

To make EGYPTIACUM.

Take Verdigreaſe in fine powder five ounces, Honey one pound, and Vinegar ſix ounces, boil the whole together until it comes to a deep Red Ointment, then ſtirred until quite cold, then for uſe. This Ointment alſo is proper for Ulcerated Wounds.

A MUSLIEGE POULTICE for BROKEN ULCERATED KNEES.

Take Green Hemlock and Foxglove of each a full handful; pound the whole together in a mortar, then add old Sour Lant and put it in a ſaucepan, and ſtew them together to the conſiſtence of a Poultice, and repeat it for ſometime to the part. The above is valuable for a Sinus on the Hough, that appears ulcerated from a ſevere bang.

An ASTRINGENT FOMENTATION.

Take Forge Water and Old Lant of each three quarts, boil therein Oak Bark a double handful, Pomegranate Bark four ounces, Bole Ammoniac four ounces, and Roch Allum two ounces; boil the whole together until it is conſumed to four quarts, then for uſe. If a Wound or Ulcer is endowed with too great a moiſture or gleet or Scrum Water, then foment the Wound or Ulcer with the above Fomentation before every dreſſing, until you ſee the ſharp humor quite abated.

To

Of ULCERS.

To Exfoliate a FOUL BONE in any ULCER.

Take Tincture of Myrrh with Aloes one ounce, and the ſtrong Tincture of Euphorbium half an ounce, mixed together for uſe: when uſed for a Foul Bone, dip a ſmall pledget of Tow in the above mixture, then apply it on the wounded Bone: then dreſs the wound up with the Mild Digeſtive Red Ointment, ſee page 89, and continue the above dreſſing until the Bone is Exfoliated clear off the part: then treat the wound as ſymptoms may appear.

A WATER to Deſtroy PROUD FLESH.

Take Corroſive Sublimate three drams, diſſolved in one quart of clear Lime Water; then for uſe. Waſh any wound with the above Water, and it will prevent Proud Fleſh from growing therein.

To Stuff and Cleanſe a FOUL ULCER.

Take Sublimate Mercury one dram, Oil of Vitriol two drams mixed together in a bottle for uſe. When uſed, take a Butcher's Skewer and wrap the end of it with Tow and dip it in the above mixture, and trace the Ulcer well withinſide, and it will cleanſe and deſtroy an Ulcer in any part. Obſerve the above application is not to be repeated only once a week or nine days and no more. Uſe the above mixture ſparingly.

The CAUSTIC PAPER to Throw out a CORE

In any part; alſo is very proper to Core a Wen or any Oozy ſubſtance whatever; alſo is very proper to ſtop a Putrified Vein that is going to mortify after bleeding. Take half a quarter of a ſheet of a News-paper, or Oozy Writing-paper, and ſpread it all over with Black Soap very thin, then ſprinkle
the

the Paper and Soap all over with Yellow Arfenic in fine powder; then roll the Paper up ftraight and level, much like unto the fhank of a tobacco-pipe, then for ufe. When ufed make four or more holes, according to the fize of the Subftance or Wen, or Vein, with a hot fmall pipe-iron, the form of a tobacco-pipe fhank, juft through the fkin; then cut the Cauftic Paper into fmall pieces about one eighth of an inch long, then put one piece of the above Paper into each hole, then fill the holes up with Black Soap, and let the whole remain in until the Core begins to crack round, then fcald the part with equal quantities of Black Pitch, Tar, and Tallow, made quite hot together and then immediately poured into the wound; repeat the fcalding every other day, until you fee the wound in a good way for a cure, then Nature alone will perform the cure, and obferve to let the Cores out of their own accord.

Section, 31.

Of INFLAMMATIONS and MORTIFICATIONS.

AN Inflammation often proceeds from a fevere wound ill-treated, or bad management; or when a wound has taken cold, or when improper digeftives have been made ufe of, by fome ignorant perfon; and if the above fhould be the cafe, a Mortification will foon appear. The fymptoms of a Mortification are as follow: the Inflammation will drop fudden, and affuage away from the place where the wound is; then the edges of the wound will feel cold, and there will appear to run a thin ferum ftinking Water from the wound:

and

and if so, the symptoms of death will soon appear. Then on the other hand if a wound should happen to a Horse when his blood and juices are in a bad habit; let the wound be ever so slight it generally proves mortal, let what will be done at it; but however symptoms might prove better; as so, make use immediately of the following Fomentation.

The FOMENTATION for an INFLAMMATION.

Take Marsh Mallows, Common Mallows, and Fox-gloves, Wormwood, Rosemary, Hemlock, Camomile, and St. John's Wort, of each a double handful; boil the above well in a sufficient quantity of grounds of Beer and Old Lant: then foment the part well with the above; and after every fomenting rub the part well with Spirits of Wine, and Camphire, to keep the part warm: then immediately, give inwardly as follows. Take Jesuit Bark and Nitre Salts of each half an ounce, and mix them together for one dose. Give two or three of the above doses every day, mixed in a quart of Watergruel. But if you should judge the blood and juices to be in a very bad habit, give as follows. Take Turbith Mineral one dram, Diapente one ounce, and Castile Soap one ounce, made up into a ball with Honey for one dose. Give the first ball as above-directed; but observe to give in the second ball and so-forth, only half a dram of Turbith Mineral, in the ensuing doses: the above to be repeated every other morning; and eight or ten of the above balls to be given. Keep warm, with Mashes and warm Water during the whole time of the above symptoms, and make use of a loose warm stable all the time.

Of MORTIFICATIONS.

An EMBROCATION for an INFLAMMATION.

Take Spirits of Wine one pint; diffolve therein Camphire two ounces, then put the whole into a quart bottle, and fill the bottle up with the beft fharp Vinegar; then for ufe. Bathe the part with the above, three times a-day: or if the part will admit of bandages, make ufe of the Vegeto Mineral Water; keep wet bandages, conftantly to the part, that have been wetted with the Vegeto Mineral Water, which is prepared as follows.

The VEGETO MINERAL WATER for an INFLAMMATION.

Take the Extract of Saturn four meat-fpoonfuls, and eight meat-fpoonfuls of ftrong Spirits of Wine ftrongly camphorated, mixed together in a quart bottle, then fill the bottle up with Spring Water, then for ufe. If the above doth not anfwer make ufe as follows.

To Stop a MORTIFICATION.

Take Train Oil one point, Oil of Turpentine half a pint, Oil of Vitriol one ounce, and Aquafortis one ounce, mixed together for ufe: then immediately rub the above mixture on the part well with your hand, and if there be a wound, apply tents of the fame application to it. The above will return a Mortification, in one dreffing, if not too far-gone; and feldom or ever fails a cure.

A POULTICE to Stop an ULCER or TUMOR, that is going to MORTIFY.

Take the beft fmall Cut Tobacco, and Birth-wort, of each two ounces in fine powder: moiften the above with half a pint of Red-port Wine; then made into a Poultice with Rye Flour.

Of STRAINS in the LOINS.

Flour. If you should want the Poultice larger, then double the quantities, and add to the above Poultice a very little Hogs-lard. By repeating the above Poultice once or twice a-day, will fuck and burst any Tumor and core it, and heal it up firm if repeated.

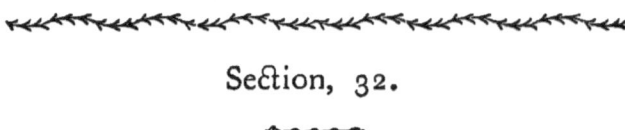

Section, 32.

Of WRENCHES or STRAINS in the BACK or LOINS.

THE symptoms of the above are well known to all men that have had the least of practice among Horses; therefore I think it needless to give a description thereof. If fresh Strains in the above part, first bleed in the Thigh Veins, then make use of the first Ball set down in the section upon hurts and gravel in the kidneys, see page 50, then immediately make use as follows. Take Spirits of Wine, and Camphire, Spirits Sal Ammoniac, and Ointment of Marsh Mallows, of each two ounces, mixed together cold for use: then rub the part well with the above mixture; then apply on the part a fresh-stripped Sheep-skin, and lay it on the Loins immediately whilst hot with the fleshy side to the part; then bind and confine the Skin on the part for forty-eight hours; then repeat the same, as above directed in all respects, in forty-eight hours to come; so repeat according as you see occasion. If the above doth not answer make use of the following.

Take Hard Spring Water and dash it upon the Loins, for half an hour together, by filling of garden watering-pots, and
pouring

pouring the Water on the Loins: then wet as much Hay with Spring Water as will cover the Loins, about a quarter of a yard thick, then lay a double blanket on the part, with proper girths to keep the hay and blanket on the part: repeat the Watering and the wet Hay every day for a-week together. The above method will fweat the part much if repeated. Then proceed as follows; take Butterton's Water, fee page 129, and rub the Loins well with the above mixture once a-day, until the part begins to fweat and become fcurfy: then leave off rubbing until the part becomes cool; then apply on the part afflicted, the Strengthening Charge, fee page 113. Then make ufe of a loofe ftable for the fpace of three months, and at the fame time give two or three cooling Purges: I would recommend the Quick Cooling Purge for an Inflamed Bowel, fee page 19.

Section, 33.

Of the SCAB or MANGE.

THE Scab is well known to all men that have had the leaft practice among Horfes, therefore its needlefs to give a defcription of it: but however, the cafe of the Scab is, if not catched from another Horfe, is generally from poverty and lownefs of blood, and in that cafe the pores of the fkin are ftagnated and void of perfpiration, which often is occafioned, by being over-heated and too fuddenly cooled, fo the poor Horfe is certain to have a bad Surfeit, if not the Scab. As the above diforder is a lurker in the fkin, outward applications

Of the SCAB.

cations are the chief cure; with the help of some inward medicines; which are to be given in the recovery of the disorder.

The OINTMENT for the SCAB or MANGE.

Take Fresh Butter one pound, Venice Turpentine one ounce, Oil of Turpentine two ounces, Quicksilver four ounces, and Black Soap four ounces; mix the Quicksilver and both of the Turpentines well together in a mortar, until the Mercury disappears to the eye, then add the Black Soap and Butter: observe to rub the Ointment a long time, until thoroughly incorporated, then for use. Rub the Horse all over with the above Ointment in the sun or by a fire, and observe to rub the Ointment well in. The above quantity is sufficient to dress two Horses. Do not stir the Horse out for four or five days, lest the effect of the Ointment should cause him to purge or slaver.

Another OINTMENT for the SCAB.

Take sharp pointed Dock-roots one pound, and boil them well in a quart of Vinegar; then bruise the Roots in a mortar, and pulp them through a hair-sieve; then add to the pulp, Black Brimstone, Gunpowder and Glass powdered, of each four ounces, and Oil of Turpentine two ounces, mixed all together in a mortar, with as much Hogs-lard as will make the whole into a slippery Ointment, then for use. Dress and rub the Horse all over with the above Ointment in the sun or by a fire. Either of the above Ointments will cure the Scab or Mange.

A MIXTURE to Wash a SCORBUTIC SCAB.

Take one quart of Lime Water, add to it Black Hellebore two ounces in fine powder, and Sublimate Mercury two drams,

drams, all mixed together in a bottle for use. Wash the part afflicted with the above mixture, according as you see occasion require. The above Mixture is very proper to wash a Horse with, after the use of the two former Ointments. Then observe in the latter part of the above disorder, to give Liver of Antimony one pound, Æthiops Mineral four ounces, Brimstone and Nitre of each half a pound mixed together: give of the above powders two ounces every day on a Mash of Bran and Oats. Then it will be proper to give a gentle purge or two after the above medicines are operated, I would recommend some of the Alterative Purges, see page 22. If the Horse is of value I would advise the owner to get him into a Salt Marsh for a month in the spring of the year, which will renew and refresh him much.

Section, 34.

Of LICE and VERMINE.

TAKE the Mercurial Ointment, see page 68, and dress sparingly with the Ointment underneath the mane and topping, and a dab here and there, or at least where you see most Lice and Vermine; do not rub much of the Ointment on, but rub it well in. Do not take the Horse out for three or four days, lest the effect of the Ointment should cause him to purge or slaver.

To Destroy LICE or VERMINE.

Take Stavesacre, otherwise called Lice Powder four ounces, Hogs-lard one pound; mix the above together in a mortar cold;

cold; then for use. This Ointment is to be used as the above in all respects: and one good dressing is sufficient for a cure.

Another to Kill LICE on a HORSE or COW.

Take the Herb Foxglove, two or three double handfuls; boil them well in six quarts of Old Lant, when almost cold, wash the Horse all over with the above decoction two or three times, that is, once a-day: the above is very safe to destroy vermine; and will cause a Horse or Cow to thrive, and come on well after it; and is proper to wash a Horse with, after he is dressed with the Ointment for the Mange; it also, is proper to wash a Horse that is subject to wet itchings in the skin, or the dry Scurvy that causes a Horse to itch, rub, and scrub, with wet blotches on the skin, that appear like unto a Tetter-worm.

Section, 35.

Of Fresh CRUSHES from the SADDLE.

TAKE Spirits of Wine and Camphire, and Oil of Turpentine, of each half a pint, and Horse Oil one pint, mixed together in a bottle for use. Rub the part afflicted with the above for half an hour together, then cover it up with hot Horse-muck out of the mixen, and repeat the same once a-day. The above will mollify the swelling and shrink it flat if not too badly crushed withinside, and if crushed badly, it will bring it to a head: then it might be cut open and treated as a Green Wound or Ulcer.

Or

Or this for the SAME.

Take Soft Soap and Brandy, and rub the part afflicted, first with the one and then with the other, for six or eight times each of them, then cover that part up with hot Horse-muck out of the mixen and a blanket.

Another for the SAME.

Take Oil of Turpentine and Linseed Oil of each half a pint, Saltpetre in fine powder two ounces, Oil of Camomile two ounces, Oil of Petre one ounce, and Roch Allum in fine powder one ounce, all mixed together for use. Rub the part afflicted with the above and cover it up, as before directed. And if the above doth not disperse the swelling you may depend that the part is collecting or forming matter underneath, and if so, you must open the part, the best way for a drain to discharge the matter off. Then treat the wound in all respects as a Green Wound or Ulcer; as I have mentioned before in the Section upon Wounds in General, see page 81, and observe the precautions there mentioned, in all respects.

Section, 36.

Of DISEASES of the EYES.

AS for Hurts or Bites and Wounds in the Eyes, they are all as accidents, and must be treated as symptoms appear; but as for Rheums and Inflammations, they all proceed from the infirmity of the Eyes: such as Moon-eyes and Cataracts. The Moon-eyes are great staring goggling Eyes, and as they are ruled by the ebb and flow of the Moon, they see better

better in a dark night, than they do in the clear day-time. And as for Cataracts or Gutta-ferena; I will not pretend to have any thing to do with either of the above infirmities, but fo far as this, I will venture to fay that a Cataract and Gutta-ferena, both end in blindnefs, and are incurable: but in the firft ftage of the above complaints, take blood, in all refpects, more or lefs, according to the fymptoms of the diforder, then make ufe as follows.

For an INFLAMED HUMOR in the EYES.

Take Skim-milk three half pints, Spring Water half a pint, and Brandy four meat-fpoonfuls, mixed together for ufe.— When ufed, make the above hot, and bathe the Eyes well, three times a-day with it, and it will cool the inflammation much.

A Famous EYE-WATER.

Take Camphire one ounce, diffolved in as much Spirits of Wine as will diffolve it, and no more; then take White Sugar Candy and White Copperas, and Fine Honey, of each two ounces, Sugar of Lead one ounce, then put the whole into a large bafon, to which add one quart of Spring Water, then ftir it for four days, four times a-day, then bottle it for ufe; and when ufed, fhake the mixture well, and if ufed for a Humor in the Eye, add half and half of Spring Water to it; and if ufed for a Film, or Speck, make ufe of the mixture itfelf without Water; and when ufed only wet your finger and draw it over the Eyelids, and ufe no Linen-cloth to the Eye.

For a WOUND in the EYE.

Take prepared Tutty one ounce, Blood-ftone prepared two fcruples, and the beft Aloes twenty-four grains; put the whole into a mortar, and mix it up into an Ointment, with a sufficient quantity of Viper's Fat, then for use. Dress the Eye twice a-day with the above Ointment, with a feather, and if the inflammation is great, wet four or five doubles of Linen-cloths, in the Vegeto Mineral Water, and keep the Eye covered with the same, and observe to renew and wet the cloths in the same Vegeto Mineral Water, four or five times a-day. The above method will cool the inflammation much. The Vegeto Mineral Water is proper for an inflammation in the Eyes, to bathe and wash the Eyes with, and is one of the best Eye-waters for an inflammation or rheum. The Vegeto Mineral Water is prepared as follows.

The VEGETO MINERAL WATER for the EYES.

Take the Extract of Saturn one meat-spoonful, and four meat-spoonfuls of Brandy; put the above into a quart bottle; then fill the bottle up with Spring Water for use. Also Rowels and Issues are proper to assist rheums and inflammations in the Eyes: and in the above case, observe not to give any hard food, that will cause labour to grind and disturb the temples or the net of the Eye; but give all as can be as food, soft and easy chewing, such as scalded Bran and Oats or boiled Barley and the like: such food is the most proper in the above case.

To take a FILM or SPECK off an EYE.

Take Red Rose-water half a pint, White Vitriol two drams, and burnt Allum two drams all in fine powder; then add six meat-spoonfuls of the Juice of Salendine; then mixed all together for use: put a little of the above into the Eye with a feather twice a-day.

For a BRUISED EYE.

Take Eyebright, Salendine and Rosemary of each a single handful, bruised together in a mortar, and Rosin in fine powder half an ounce; boil the above in a pint of Fresh Cream over a slow fire, then strain it off for use. Put some of the above Ointment into the Eye with a feather twice a-day; and also smear the Eyelid over with the same. If the blood and juices are in a bad habit, all the outward applications avail nothing, therefore you must have recourse to inward medicines, I would recommend the Turbith Mineral Ball, see page 24, or give gentle physic, or a course of Liver of Antimony and Flour of Brimstone, and Nitre Salts, of each the same quantity, mixed together and given in all his Mashes; that is, one meat-spoonful on a Mash twice a-day.

Section, 37.

Of the VIVES.

THE Vives is a swelling of the Glands and Vive-cord, which lieth underneath the Ears, and proceedeth downwards to the Gullet or Valve: In a young Horse, it doth not require much more than bleeding and keeping warm for the time; but if the above complaint should happen to an old Horse, it denotes a crazy constitution, which is but seldom got clear of. The above generally seizes a Horse, when at Grass. As so, observe to keep him up for some time, then proceed as follows.

For

Of the VIVES.

For the VIVES on a YOUNG HORSE.

First bleed, then take Spirits of Wine strongly camphorated, and Marsh Mallows Ointment of each two ounces, mixed together cold, then for use. Rub the part well with the above Ointment; then cover it up with hot Horse-muck out of the mixen; then put on his head a cap-hood to confine the muck to the part. Repeat the same once a-day, and give Nitre Salts in all his Mashes and warm Water, during the time of his illness.

For the VIVES on an OLD HORSE.

First bleed, and order him in all respects at first, as above for a young Horse; then after the inflammation is abated, rub the Vive-cord twice a-day, with the strong Mercurial Quicksilver Ointment, see page 68, until the substance is quite dispersed, and the part becomes flat and mellow: and if the above doth not shrink the part quite flat, you must proceed as follows. Blister the part two or three times, or at least until the part is quite reduced fine; and be sure to give time between each of the Blisters, for the part to cool and become clear from scurf, before you repeat another Blister: you may make use of the Mild Blister, see page 108. Then it would be proper to get some safe skilful hand to lay the firing iron on the part; then apply the Strengthening Charge, see page 113, and let it remain on for six weeks at least, observing not to turn him to Grass; for the hanging down of the head is very hurtful to the disorder. Then give him Liver of Antimony, Nitre Salts and Flour of Brimstone on all his Mashes: or if he is a Horse of value it would be proper to give him three or four doses of gentle Physic, I would recommend some of the Alterative Purges, see page 22.

Section,

Section, 38.

Of Bad NECKS and VEINS after BLEEDING.

AS all men, in and out of practice, are acquainted with the above more or less, therefore it needs no further explanation of the symptoms thereof. At the first stage of the above, make use as follows.

Take Nerve Ointment one ounce, and Oil of Amber one ounce, mix the above together cold for use, then rub the part well with the above mixture, then heat it in with a hot iron, and repeat the above dressing once a-day, or as occasion may require the use of it.

For VEINS that swell after BLEEDING.

Take equal parts of Soft Soap and Brandy, made hot together in a cup or pan, and stirred until it comes to a slippery Ointment, then immediately whilst hot, rub the part well with the above mixture, then heat it in with a hot iron.

The above dressing will cause the part to swell much, and will bring on a strong scurf: when the swelling is abated from the effect of the above dressing, repeat the same in all respects, as above directed.

For VEINS that swell after BLEEDING.

Take the Firing Ointment, see page 131, and rub the part well with it, then heat it in with a hot iron and observe to keep him from rubbing the part, for the above dressing will caufe the part to fwell and fweat much. When the fwelling and fweating abates, and the part is become clear from fcurf, from the effect of the above drefling, repeat the above in all refpects, as above-mentioned. Then on the other hand, if the Vein is corded hard and callous, and feems to be putrified, and doth appear to creep up to the vives or glands: then make ufe as follows. Obferve to ftrike a fleam into the corded vein right upon the part where he was bled: make four holes with the fleam, in the compafs of a fhilling-piece; then take Yellow Arfenic, about the fize of a fmall pea, in fine powder, mix with it about twice as much Black Soap; put the whole on the fleamed part and temper it well in, with the point of a knife, and fo let it remain on: and if the Vein is much fwelled, and corded hard, you muft fleam it in two or three places more, as before directed, and be fure to make one of the incifions at the upper part of the putrified Vein, in order to ftop it, before it gets up to the Glands or Vives; then apply the Arfenic and Black Soap as before directed, upon every fleamed part: then tie his head up to the rack for fome days, and be fure to keep him from rubbing the part.

The above application will caufe a core or fubftance to come out of each part that was fleamed and cauftic. When the part begins to crack around, fcald it with equal parts of Black Pitch, Tar, and Tallow made quite fcalding-hot together, and then dafhed or poured into the wounds. Obferve to fcald the part every other day. As fo, continue until fuch time as the core comes out: then omit the fcalding; that is, once every fourth day; then nature alone will perform the cure. Or the following cauftic may be ufed inftead of the above, which will penetrate deeper.

Take

Take the Cauſtic Paper, ſee page 91, and make uſe of it in all reſpects as there directed, on all occaſions.

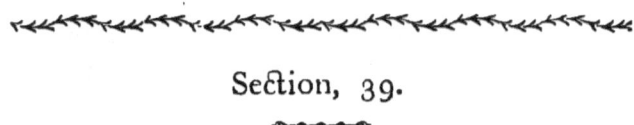

Section, 39.

Of a CANKER in the MOUTH and TAIL.

TAKE Sharp Vinegar one quart, Brier Leaves and Red Sage of each a ſingle handful, boiled together, then add Roch Allum in powder one ounce, Honey three ounces, and Bole Ammoniac in fine powder two ounces, all boiled together for uſe. Waſh the Mouth twice a-day with the above, with the aſſiſtance of a linen rag tied to the end of a ſtick.

For a CANKER in the MOUTH.

Take Sublimate Mercury two drams, and put it into a quart bottle full of Spring Water, and let it ſtand for two or three days; then for uſe. Waſh the Horſe's Mouth with the above twice a-day as the former directs you in all reſpects.

The above Water is very proper to waſh a man or woman's mouth, as a gargle for a ſore throat or mouth: either a man or woman may ſwallow a tea-ſpoonful with ſafety; but when uſed for human bodies, take one dram of Sublimate Mercury inſtead of two. The above Water will cauſe to void phlegm when no other application will: a ſucking child may ſwallow ſix or eight drops in a tea-ſpoonful of Spring Water with ſafety.

For a CANKER in the TAIL.

Take Hogs-lard one pound, and Oil of Vitriol one ounce, mixed together in a mortar, into a blackiſh or grey Ointment, then

then for ufe. If it fhould be the Wet Canker, rub the part with the above fparingly, but if it is the Dry Canker, rub the part plentifully. Alfo, the above Ointment anfwers well to ftop a heat, that frequently happens to a Tail, on the upper part when in the pullies in the time of fetting, and fo-forth, by only fmearing fome of the Ointment with your finger on the galled part of the Tail.

Section, 40.

****

Of BLISTERS of VARIOUS SORTS.

BLISTERS are proper for all hard Excrefcences, and hard callous Subftances, and for let or broken-down Sinews, and Spavins, Ringbones, Curbs and Splents, and alfo do affift to difperfe all hard Tumors, fuch as have no matter formed in them. By repeating any of the following Blifters, as occafion may require the ufe of them.

A MILD BLISTER.

Take the Quickfilver Oil of Bays two ounces, Cantharides, Euphorbium, and Oil of Origanum, of each two drams, all mixed together for ufe. The above is mild in its operation, and might be made ufe of with fafety where a Blifter is required, obferving to give proper intervals between each Blifter, that the part may become cool and clear from fcurf before you repeat another Blifter.

The

Of BLISTERS.

The VITRIOL BLISTER.

Take Hogs-lard eight ounces, Oil of Vitriol one ounce, Cantharides one ounce, Roman Vitriol in fine powder three ounces, Oil of Turpentine one ounce, all mixed together for ufe.

The above Blifter is proper for a relaxed Sinew, or any hard Excrefcence whatever, and may be repeated as you fee occafion, or at leaft when you fee the part clear from fcurf, and the inflammation quite abated.

A Strong BLISTER for a Let-down SINEW.

Take Oil of Bays with Quickfilver three ounces, Cantharides and Euphorbium of each one dram, Sublimate Mercury one dram, Yellow Arfenic one dram, all in fine powder, and Oil of Origanum two drams, all mixed together for ufe.

Rub the Sinew well with the above; and repeat it as occafion may require the ufe of it, but is not to be repeated until the part is clear from fcurf, and the inflammation quite abated; the above Blifter is not to be heated in with a hot iron.

The BLISTER after FIRING.

Take Bees-wax, Horfe Turpentine and Hogs-lard, of each two ounces; melt the above together, then add Oil of Turpentine one ounce, Train Oil fix ounces, then add carefully Oil of Vitriol one ounce, Bole Ammoniac in fine powder two ounces, all mixed together, and keep ftirring it until cold.

The above to be fpread on the fired part with a knife once only and no more, and is not to be heated in with a hot iron; then tie his head up for three or four days and nights, then let

let him be put into a loose stable for three weeks, then to grafs for three months at least.

A BLISTER for a SHOULDER-STRAIN.

Take Nerve Oil and Hogs-lard of each three ounces, Common Tar two ounces, Cantharides and Sublimate Mercury of each two drams, and Oil of Turpentine one ounce, all mixed together for one dose.

Rub the part afflicted well with the above; and repeat the same when you see the part clear from scurf and the inflammation quite abated.

The STRONG LIQUID BLISTER.

Take Oil of Petre one ounce, Oil of Vitriol two drams, Oil of Origanum one ounce and a half, Cantharides and Euphorbium of each two drams and Sublimate Mercury in fine powder two drams, all mixed together in a bottle for use.

Rub and dab the part afflicted, and no where else, with the above three times in the space of one hour, and repeat it as you see occasion, but not to be repeated until the inflammation is quite abated and the part is clear from scurf. The above is proper for Splents and Spavins. First bruise the part gently with a blood-stick, then dress it with the above, as above directed.

The Strong BLISTER for a BONE-SPAVIN.

Take Euphorbium, Sublimate Mercury, Black Hellebore, Cantharides, Quicksilver, and Flour of Brimstone, of each one

Of BLISTERS.

one ounce; firſt kill the Quickſilver and the Brimſtone together in a mortar, until the Mercury diſappears to the eye; then add to the above, Quickſilver Oil of Bays two ounces, Common Tar two ounces, and Oil of Origanum half an ounce, all mixed together for uſe. Let this be repeated as you ſee occaſion; but not until the part is clear from ſcurf and the inflammation quite abated.

A Milder BLISTER for a BONE-SPAVIN.

Take Nerve Oil, Marſh Mallows Ointment, and Quickſilver of each two ounces; kill the Quickſilver, with one ounce of Venice Turpentine, until the Mercury diſappears to the eye; then add Cantharides and Euphorbium of each two drams, then mix all together for uſe.

When the above or the former is uſed; firſt bruiſe the part gently with a blood-ſtick until it feels ſoft; then apply on the Spavin a ſtrong coat of the above, and temper it in with the point of a knife, juſt as wide as the Spavin-part is and no wider; to be repeated as occaſion may require the uſe of it.

Obſerve in the above Bliſters to give proper intervals between each Bliſter for the part to become cool and clear from ſcurf before another is repeated, and ſo-forth.

Section,

Section, 41.

Of CHARGES.

The BLISTERING CHARGE.

TAKE Oxycroceum, Paracelcus, Horfe Turpentine, Burgundy Pitch, Bees-wax, Affafœtida, ftrained Galbanum, Maftic, and Dragons Blood of each two ounces, Black Pitch and Rofin of each four ounces, Aquafortis, Oil of Origanum, Euphorbium, and Cantharides, of each two drams; melt all the Gums firft together over a flow fire; when melted and the fermentation is over, put the cauftics in by a little at a time, and ftir them well together for ufe.

The above is a good Strengthening Charge; but when ufed as a Strengthening Charge; obferve to leave out the Aquafortis, Oil of Origanum, Cantharides, and Euphorbium; then the above will anfwer the intention of a Strengthening Charge in all refpects.

A Stimulating CHARGE *or* SEARCLOTH.

Take Burgundy Pitch one pound, ftrained Galbanum two ounces, Camphire one ounce and a half, melt the two firft articles together over a flow fire, when it begins to cool put in the Camphire in fine powder, ftir it all together, then pour it into Water, then draw it and form it into Rolls for ufe; then apply it as a Charge in all refpects on any part. The above is a good Searcloth for man or woman.

The

The COLD CHARGE.

Take Verjuice half a pint, and the white of two or three Eggs; beat them well together in a cup, then add Brandy one gill; mix the above together, and add Bole Ammoniac two ounces in fine powder, and as much Blue Clay, dried and made into fine powder, as will make the whole into a due confiftence of a Charge, then for ufe.

The above is a great ftrengthener and cooler, for a relaxed weak Sinew; and is to be fpread thick upon the Sinew, and covered with a fheet of Brown Paper; then fwaddle the Leg round with a Flannel Roller. The above to be repeated once a-day: this is of infinite fervice to affuage inflammations, and greatly relieves any relaxed or diftreffed joint whatever, by applying as above directed.

Section, 42.

****

Of the POLL-EVIL and FISTULA.

THE Poll-evil and Fiftula, are to be treated alike, and what will cure the one will cure the other. The Poll-evil is a lurking Sinus or Bag, fituated on each fide of the great Tendon on the top of the Poll of the Head, and traces from fide to fide underneath the great Tendon, and is generally full of a curdy or bony matter. The Fiftula is a lurking Sinus or Bag, on each fide of the Withers, rather forward towards the Neck than not.

If there should be matter formed, in either of the above calamities, I would advise by no means to stop it from coming to a head, for by such practice they become to have poking stiff heads and necks: and on the other hand it generally ends in death; but if there should be a wound on the Withers from the Saddle, you must treat it as a Green Wound or Ulcer in all respects, see page 81, and if there should be an Ulcer or Cavity, and necessity should urge you to open it; then cut the Ulcer the whole length of the Cavity, the best way for a drain to discharge the matter off, then treat the Wound as above directed; on the other hand if either of the above calamities, in the first stage should seem to be soft and limpy with no matter formed in them, you may make use of the following Applications, which I think is the best and only way to stop it safe, and not danger a Horse's life in doing of it.

To Stop the POLL-EVIL or FISTULA when Young.

First bleed, then set in three Rowels, one in the Breast and two underneath the Belly, then cut the hair off the part: then take the Firing Ointment, see page 131, and rub the part well with it for half an hour, then heat it in with a hot iron.

The above will cause the part to swell and sweat much, and will bring on a strong scurf: then give proper time for the scurf to clear off, of itself; then observe to repeat the Ointment again, if occasion be, in all respects as above directed. When the scurf is clear off the part, after the last dressing with the Ointment, lay the Blistering Charge on, see page 112, and let it remain on as long as possible.

Also,

Of the POLL-EVIL.

Alſo, to Stop the POLL-EVIL or FISTULA when Young.

Take the Black Oils, ſee page 130, and make uſe of them in all reſpects, as the latter Receipt directs you. If the above methods do not perform a cure, and the Poll-evil or Fiſtula is got quite to a head, and full of matter; then obſerve to make uſe as follows.

Never cut either of the above diſorders, except the part is quite ripe and full of matter; then cut it, and obſerve, let this be a rule in all your cutting of the above diſorder; that is, to cut the Sinus length-ways, but never croſs-ways; and obſerve to cut the Sinus or Cavity quite to the bottom, and leave none of the Cavities uncut open, when that is over, cram the Ulcer full of Tow dipped in Oil of Turpentine: then immediately make uſe of the following Ointment, and that made quite ſcalding hot; then take the Tow out, and pour the following Ointment, whilſt ſcalding hot, into the Ulcer; firſt obſerving to ſtretch the Ulcer open, with the Trowel Iron made for that purpoſe, in order to receive the Ointment into the bottom of the Ulcer, the form of the Trowel Iron, is much like a Bricklayer's Trowel, when that is over, do not ſuffer the Ulcer to be dreſſed with any application at all for three weeks.

The above method, commonly performs a cure. Then in three weeks time, if there ſhould be no ſymptoms of a cure, you muſt cut the Ulcer again, and repeat as above-mentioned in all reſpects.

But if the Poll-evil or Fiſtula when cut, ſhould prove petrified withinſide and full of corroded Bones, make uſe as follows, inſtead of the Scald or Oinment.

Take

Of the POLL-EVIL.

Take Tincture of Myrrh with Aloes two ounces, the strong Tincture of Euphorbium two ounces, Oil of Turpentine two ounces, Sublimate Mercury three drams in fine powder, all mixed together for use; when used shake the mixture well, and wet a strong pledget of Tow with the above mixture, then thrust the pledget into the bottom of the Wound, and let it remain in for six days; then renew it every six days, and continue the dressings until the Bones are exfoliated clear out of the Ulcer; then if needful, make use of the following Ointment, as the under-mentioned directs you in all respects.

The following is the Scald or Ointment.

The POLL-EVIL or FISTULA OINTMENT.

Take of the best Common Tar three pounds, Mutton Suet of the Loin-part three pounds, the best and clearest Black Pitch three pounds, Bees-wax three pounds, and Black Rosin three pounds, melt the above all together; then stirred until quite cold, then for use. When used either for the Poll-evil or Fistula, after cutting, observe never to make use of less than one pound at one time, and that always made quite scalding hot: then immediately poured fuzzing hot into the Ulcer or Wound, after cutting, as before directed. The above method originally, came from old Kidney, but since, in my practice, it has undergone some practical alterations of mine in several respects.

Another SCALD for the POLL-EVIL or FISTULA.

If the above calamity requires to be cut the third time, make use as follows. Take Verdigrease two ounces in fine powder, Sublimate Mercury four drams, Train Oil one pint, Oil of Turpentine half a pint, and Oil of Vitriol two ounces,

all

all mixed together for use. If the second cutting and dressing fails a cure, make use of the above Oils for the third dressing, after cutting. Use the above in all respects, as the latter Ointment, that is, to be made quite hot, and pour it into the Wound.

For an Obstinate Petrified POLL-EVIL or FISTULA.

First draw a circle around the substance with the Firing-iron almost through the skin; then within the circle, make ten or fifteen regular holes with an Iron, about the size of the shank of a Tobacco-pipe; observe to burn each hole through the skin about the depth of a Barley-corn, then apply into each hole, a piece of Yellow Arsenic, the size of a small grain of Wheat, and lap a little paper about each piece of Arsenic; then fill each hole up with Black Soap. The above method will cause a great core or substance to come out of the part in about three weeks time. Then observe to scald the part every other day, with equal quantities of Black Pitch, Tar and Tallow, made quite scalding hot together, then immediately poured into the Wound or Ulcer: then after the substance comes off the part, and there should be a Cavity remaining, wash the part with the Sublimate Water, see page 91, then nature alone will perform the cure.

To Destroy an ULCER or SINUS that Remains in a POLL-EVIL or FISTULA.

Take Oil of Vitriol two drams, Sublimate Mercury one dram, in powder, mixed together in a small bottle for use, and when used, take a stiff small Probe or a Butcher's Skewer, wrap a little Tow round the end of the Skewer, then dip it well in the above mixture, then put it into the Ulcer and work it well all round withinfide of the Cavities. The above will flough and cleanfe the Wound much; the above not to be repeated for nine days to come, nor feldom requires any more drefling.

Section, 43.

Of LAMPAS and WOLVES TEETH and FLAPS in the MOUTH.

THE Lampas is an Excrefcence in the Roof of the Mouth, fo that upon opening the Mouth you may perceive that the Roof or firft bar of the Mouth appears above the fore Teeth. The above is common to all young Horfes: I have feen feveral young Horfes, at two or three, or four years old, to have the Lampas as fome people call it; but to the beft of my memory, I never took the Lampas out of any of our own Horfes; fo all men that will take notice of a young Horfe's Mouth, will always find his Teeth fhort, and that is the reafon that the Roof of the Mouth appears higher than the Teeth: but if a fix or feven years old Horfe has the Lampas, you may take the firft bar of the Roof of his Mouth off, with a hot iron made for that purpofe; then nature will perform the cure.

The Wolves Teeth are fhort ftumpy Teeth, which are fituated up to the Grinders of the upper Jaw, they are very hurtful to the Eyes, and the fooner they are taken out the better; the method of taking them out is as follows. Get a
narrow

narrow chifel punch with a crane neck and a fmall forked end. Then fet the forked end of the punch to the root of the Tooth, with the crane neck projecting upwards, and fo, hit the haft of the chifel fmartly with a mallet, which method will take the Tooth out; then nature alone will perform the cure.

The Flaps are a fpungy, flefhy, fungous fubftance, fituated juft below the Grinders on the lower Jaw, adjoining the cheek, on the part where the Bit refteth upon. The above is fo troublefome to a Horfe and fo fore, that he will often catch the Flaps between his Grinders, which chafes him much, and prevents him to grind his food, and caufes him to flaver and flobber much.

In the above cafe, firft clip all the fpungy part clear away with a pair of fciffors, and then rub the part well with Common Salt; then nature alone will perform the cure. The above methods always ferved me, on the above occafions.

Section, 44.

Of ORNAMENTS in General, or rather to be termed SKILFUL OPERATIONS, that are commonly performed and practifed on HORSES.

I Shall not dwell upon all particulars of the above word, Ornament, but fhall fet down what has ferved my purpofe, and leave it to all men of fkill, to practife as others have done before them.

Firft of fetting of Ears, as follows.

Of ORNAMENTS.

Of SETTING of EARS.

In the first place take the superfluous skin away, that lieth from the nape of the Head to the division of the Mane, and also down to the root of the Ear, and three inches upwards towards the point of the Ear: take all that skin away with a pair of scissors and a knife, then bathe the flayed part with Rum, then stitch the edges of the skin close together, and apply a plaister all over the stitched part, as follows.

Take the Yolk of two Eggs, Honey two ounces, and Bole Ammoniac three ounces, in fine powder, mixed together; then applied on the part, plaister-ways spread on a linen-cloth; then take two stiff tents made with wheat straw, and wrapped round with linen-cloth, much in the form of a large case-knife's haft; dip the tents in a batter made of the Whites of Eggs and Wheat Flour, and set them in the Ears; then set on a leather cap-hood made for that purpose, which is to remain on for a month at least, and must not be shifted during the whole time.

Of CROPPING of EARS.

The art of Cropping is but simple to a man that knows some little of that way of Business. In the first place, cut the Ears as nigh nature as you can, then draw the skin up tight and pin it through the gristle with five or six pins; then if there should be any superfluous skin remaining, pare it off close to the gristle with a pair of scissors; then dab and wash the Ears with Rum, and keep him in for four days; then take the pins out, then turn him into a loose stable, and there let him be until he is got well of his ears; on the other hand, there are some people that make use of Ear-pieces and Engines, but they

Of ORNAMENTS.

they that know the art of cropping, can do as well without the pieces as with them, as the Ears commonly are to be altered after the pieces are taken off.

To make a STAR.

Take a ſtick of tough Sealingwax, and warm the end of it at a candle; then dab the part where you mean to have the Star on with the Wax; then take a Butcher's Skewer about four inches long, and lay it on the waxed part, then dab and cover the Skewer with the Wax; then take a halfpenny ball of Packthread and wind it tight about the Skewer, and gather the hair with the ſtring, and the Wax ſtill warmed at a candle, and continue to gather the hair with the Wax as you go round with the ſtring, ſo that the ſtring and the hair, and the Wax may lay hold of each other: then wet the ſtring twice that day with cold Water, and let the ſtring remain on two days and two nights.

Then take off the ſtring and the ſkewer, and apply on a plaiſter of Black Pitch, which is to remain on a fortnight at leaſt; and in two months time, you will ſee what you wiſhed for.

Alſo to make a STAR.

Make two holes through the ſkin juſt on the part that you mean to have the Star on, one hole above and the other below, then take a ſtiff iron ſkewer and thruſt it underneath the ſkin from hole to hole; the holes are to be ſeparate from each other about three inches: then take a halfpenny ball of Packthread and wind it very tight around the ſkewer; then wet the Packthread with cold Water, and uſe the ſame precautions with this, as the latter mentions in all reſpects.

Of ORNAMENTS.

The METHOD of SETTING a TAIL.

Cut the Tail acrofs in three, or four, or five places according to art, and be fure to cut the main Sinews on each fide quite through; then weaken the fmall ligament in the middle of the Tail, and cut the ends off the main Tendon away; then wafh and dab the Wounds with Oil of Turpentine: then drefs the Wounds up with Venice Turpentine and the Yolk of an Egg, of each the fame quantity mixed together. Then apply the above to the wounds with proper pledgets and bandages, and immediately fet the Horfe in the pully: the next day flacken the bandages, but obferve to let them remain on for four days at leaft; then take the dreffing off, and obferve to make ufe of no application at all to the Wounds, but puff them full with Wheat Flour every day, or at leaft when the fcabs are off and the Wounds appear raw.

Alfo, a Good SAFE DRESSING for a TAIL after SETTING.

Take Tincture of Myrrh with Aloes, and Oil of Turpentine, of each one ounce, mixed together for ufe; then dab the Wounds with a ftrong pledget of Tow dipped in the above mixture, and bind them on with a proper bandage, and obferve the above precifion in all refpects.

Of GELDING a HORSE.

Firft obferve, when you mean to Geld a Horfe, that the figns are in the legs or feet; then get the Horfe properly caft, then wafh and clean his fheath, and liquor the part well with Goofe Oil, then take one of the Tefticles up firm between your firft finger and thumb, then bolt the Stone out of the Scrotum with your hot iron and make as wide an orifice as

you

Of ORNAMENTS.

you can; then fix your clams quite below the Tefticle, on the blood veffels and ligament, then take the Tefticle off with your hot iron juft one inch above the clams; then fear the blood veffels; but ftrictly obferving that your iron is not too hot, and be fure to ftanch the blood: then apply on the veffels, a little Goofe Oil and fear it in with your hot iron; then let go the blood veffels by a little at a time to prove whether the blood is ftanched or not, before you let them go for good.— Then do the fame with the other Tefticle in all refpects: then melt with the hot iron half a pint of Goofe Oil, and pour half of it into one orifice and the other half into the other orifice, then give the Scrotum a fhake; then put into each orifice a piece of fat Bacon, the fize of a large Egg, then ftitch the Scrotum acrofs to keep the Bacon in: then untie the Horfe and get him into a loofe warm ftable, and obferve to indulge him with Mafhes and warm Water, and gentle walking exercife, but do not take him out of the ftable until the third day, obferving not to touch the Wounds with any application at all, but what is above-mentioned.

The Method of FIRING or SCORING.

That man that doth this work, always ought to fearch the parts where the operation is intended to be, whether the part is fit for the reception of the fire, and clear from being gummy, and if fo, the fire will have the better effect. Then I fay if a Spavin, or Curb, or Ringbone, or Whirlbone, or Backfinew, or the Vives, or any other part require firing, apply the iron on according as the part requires, and obferve to draw the lines level and true, near half through the fkin, but ftrictly obferving not through the fkin, and always keep the lines or fcores about three parts of an inch diftant from each other

Of STRAINS and LAMENESS.

other, and so do the work as artful as you can; then apply on the part, the Blister after Firing, see page 109, then tie the Animal up four days and nights; then turn him into a loose stable for three weeks, then to Grass for three months at least.

Section, 45.

Of LAMENESS, STRAINS or BRUISES in the SHOULDER, WHIRLBONE, STIFLE, HOUGH, or KNEE.

FIRST of the general symptoms of Lamenesses in any of the above parts. Severe Lamenesses in any of the above parts, are very easy to be found out, but slight Lamenesses in some parts are rather nice to be pointed at, but however, I will endeavour to give an account of what served me on such occasions.

First, the symptoms of Lameness in the Fore-foot, if a Horse is lame in the Fore-foot, he will point out the Foot as he treads and never drag his toe, and will put his Foot straight out, and defend or tread very tender. On the other hand if a pain in the Foot, and you cannot find it out, put the Foot into a pail of Water for half an hour, then take it out of the Water, and watch diligently which part of the Foot becomes dry soonest: the part that dries soonest is that where the pain lieth. The same symptoms as the Fore-foot, the Coffin and Pastern have in their appearances in going or treading.

The

The symptoms of a Lameness in the Knee are, a Horse will go with a stiff Knee, and the Knee will seem to knuckle or project forward, and if badly relaxed, a severe inflammation will attend the part, and his appearance in going will be, to tuck his two Hind-legs and Feet quite forward underneath his weight, and so hanch forward and defend upon the sound Fore-leg, with his lame Knee projecting forward, and his toe seemeth always to hang back.

The symptoms of Lameness in the Elbow are, a Horse will be exceeding stiff and lame, and appear in his way of going to form a half-circle, twisting outwards with his Foot every step he goes.

The symptoms of Lameness in the Shoulder are known, by the Horse not pointing out his Leg and Foot, and appears always to tread short; and if the Lameness is great, he will drag his toe along the ground every step he goes; and if he is turned sharp round to the lame-side it will almost throw him down if not quite; and if both Shoulders, are afflicted, then humors generally attend the Chest and Shoulders, and he will appear to stammer and stumble much like to a dog that is shook in the Shoulders.

The symptoms of a Lameness in the Hough are very visible, as the Hough generally will swell upon the least relaxation or Sprain, and if persevered with work, the above case will bring on a severe inflammation.

The symptoms of a Lameness in the Stifle are, the Stifle will swell if badly relaxed; and the Stifle-joint will project and knuckle forward, and he will tread very short and just touch

touch the ground with his toe, and will not fet his heel down at all.

The fymptoms of a Lamenefs in the Whirlbone and Hip are, if a fevere Lamenefs in either of the above parts it is very eafy to find it out, but if a flight Lamenefs it is as difficult. The method to find out Lamenefs in the above parts is, to let a Horfe walk and trot for half an hour, then obferve ftrictly as he moves, and you may fee him tread with a caft, fhelving outwardly with his toe; and appear to take fhort fteps, and tread upon the infide heel, and defend quick and fhort with the found Leg.

Firft, for frefh Strains in any of the above parts, make ufe of either of the following Embrocations.

The EMBROCATION for Frefh STRAINS.

Take Spirits of Wine half a pint, and Camphire two ounces, diffolved in the above Spirits: then add Spirit of Sal Ammoniac two ounces put the above into a quart bottle, then fill the bottle up with fharp Vinegar made from either Goofeberries or Currants, then for ufe.

Rub the part well with the above twice a-day, and keep the part warm with Flannel Sweaters, and if the Lamenefs is great, firft bleed, if the part will admit of bleeding. If a fevere inflammation fhould attend the part, make ufe of the Fomentation, fee page 93, and obferve the directions there mentioned in all refpects.

Of STRAINS AND LAMENESS.

The BRINE-EMBROCATION for Fresh STRAINS.

Take Spirits of Wine and Camphire, Oil of Turpentine, old Rum, and old Verjuice of each two ounces, Beef's Brine eight ounces, all mixed and shook in a bottle well together for use.

Rub the part afflicted with the above, and repeat it as you see occasion require the use of it in all respects.

The GALL-EMBROCATION for Fresh STRAINS.

Take Spirits of Wine half a pint, and Camphire two ounces dissolved in the above Spirits; and Oil of Turpentine two ounces, put the above into a quart bottle, and add one pint of Beef's Gall, then shake the whole well together for use.

Rub the part well with the above, and keep the part warm with Flannel Rollers. Repeat the above once a-day or as you see occasion require.

After the use of either of the above Embrocations, and the pain is repelled, make use of the following Strengthener.

Take strong Beef's Brine and the grounds of old Beer, of each two quarts, Camomile and Wormwood of each a full double handful boiled well together, then bathe the part afflicted twice a-day with the above whilst hot. The repetition of the above will brace most parts firm.

Of STRAINS and LAMENESS.

The ITALIAN OILS for Fresh STRAINS in the SHOULDER or STIFLE.

Take Oil of Origanum and Oil of Wormwood of each one ounce, Oil of Petre two ounces, mixed together in a bottle for use. Rub the part sparingly with this mixture, and it will cause a flight scurf to come on the part: repeat two of the above dressings, that is one every other day.

If an obstinate Strain in either of the above parts, especially in the Stifle, make use as follows; that is, to swim the Horse in deep Water or rather in the Sea, once a day for a week together: the above method has been of great service for Lameness in the Stifle or Shoulders; also, Issues or Rowels are proper to assist the cure of Lamenesses in several parts of the body; but if an old Strain in the Shoulders, the most proper place to put a Rowel in, is on the top of the fin of the Shoulder-blade, just below the Withers: a Rowel runs in that part, and discharges more matter off than in any other part of the body whatever. At the same time make use of any of the following mixtures, if occasion requires.

A Strong MIXTURE of OILS.

Take Train Oil six ounces, Spirit of Sal Ammoniac, and Oil of Turpentine of each two ounces, and Spirits of Hartshorn, Oil of Petre, Oil of Origanum, Oil of Vitriol, of each one ounce, all mixed together; then put the whole into a quart bottle, then fill the bottle up with Strong Beer for use.

Rub the part well with the above, according as occasion may require the use of it, observing to rub it well in at all times.

Of STRAINS and LAMENESS.

The faid mixture is proper for a Strain in the Shoulder, Stifle or Whirlbone.

Another MIXTURE of OILS.

Take Oil of Turpentine fix ounces, Spirits of Hartfhorn, Spirits of Lavender and Oil of Origanum, of each one ounce, Aquafortis one ounce, Spirits of Wine and Camphire one pint, and Powder of Gum Amber two ounces levigated quite fine, all mixed together in a bottle for ufe. This mixture is recommended as the latter, in all refpects.

For a BANG in any PART.

Take Oil of Turpentine one pint, Barbadoes Tar two ounces, and Spirit of Sal Ammoniac two ounces, all mixed together for ufe. Rub the part well with the above, and keep the part warm with Flannel Rollers.

To make BUTTERTON's WATER.

Take the beft and hardeft Spring Water from the Iron Stone, five large pints, and white Arfenic in fine Powder three ounces, then mix the Arfenic and the Water together, in a clean maflin or bell-metal pot cold; then fet it over a very flow fire until boiled, and obferve only to let it boil two minutes and no more, ftirring it all the time with a wooden Splint whilft on the fire; then take it off the fire and cover it up until morning, then clear off two large quart bottles full for ufe; and throw the fediments away.

When ufed take three parts of the above Water, and one part of Oil of Turpentine and mix them together for ufe, when

when ufed, fhake the mixture well, then rub the part afflicted well with it; but obferve to ufe the mixture very fparingly.

The above mixture is for a Strain or Bruife in any joint whatever, and is one of the beft of fimples for new or old Strains in any part. Rub the part afflicted well once a-day with the above, until the part begins to fweat and fcurf, then obferve to leave off rubbing until the part becomes cool and clear from fcurf, before it is repeated.

But if the above mixture fhould prove too fevere to any part when ufed, mix with it the Gall-embrocation, fee page 127, of each a like quantity, which makes the mixture much milder, efpecially if ufed to human fpecies.

The Black OILS for OLD STRAINS.

Take Oil of Turpentine four ounces, Porpus Oil fix ounces, Oil of Petre, Venice Turpentine and Nerve Oil of each one ounce; Ointment of Marfh Mallows, Flanders Oil of Bays, and Barbadoes Tar, of each two ounces.

Melt the above all together over a flow fire, then put the whole into a quart bottle, then add Sublimate Mercury in fine Powder one ounce and a half, then fhake the whole well together for ufe.

The above is proper for old Strains in any part, or for broken-down Sinews; let the above be well rubbed on the part, and heated in with a hot iron, if ufed for the Sinews, the above will caufe the part to fwell, fweat and fcurf much; then obferve to give proper time for the part to become cool and clear from fcurf, before it is repeated; then repeat three or four of the above dreffings as above directed in all refpects.

The

Of STRAINS and LAMENESS.

The FIRING-OINTMENT for OLD STRAINS.

Take Oil of Turpentine three ounces, Spirits of Wine and Camphire three ounces, Nerve Ointment three ounces, Palm Oil three ounces, Oil of Bays with Quickſilver three ounces, Bees-wax three ounces, Burgundy Pitch three ounces, Venice Turpentine three ounces, Deer Suet eight ounces, and Hogs-lard eight ounces, melt the above all together over a ſlow fire; when melted and almoſt cold, add Sublimate Mercury three ounces, in fine powder, and Oil of Origanum two ounces; then ſtir the Ointment with a Spatula, until quite cold, then for uſe.

This Ointment is of univerſal ſervice for a Garget in a Cow's Udder, by rubbing the Udder with it, and drawing the Dugs well at the ſame time; but when the above Ointment is uſed for a Garget in a Cows Udder, obſerve to make uſe but of one ounce of the above Ointment, and add two ounces of the Ointment of Elder, then melt the above together and rub the Udder well. And there are other Sections in this Book obligated to the above Ointment, and it doth anſwer well in all that it is recommended and ſet down for; ſuch as injured Necks after bleeding, and to diſperſe hard excreſcences, and for let-down Sinews, and to ſtop the Poll-evil, and Fiſtula, and other maladies of thoſe kinds.

To Eaſe a Severe PAIN on any JOINT, from a Bad BANG or BRUISE.

Take Oil of Origanum one ounce, Pure Oil of Petre one ounce, Tincture of Opium two drams, mixed together for uſe; rub the part twice a-day well, but be very ſparing with the mixture; keep the part warm with a Flannel Roller, and ſo repeat it.

Of STRAINS and LAMENESS.

My OPODELDOC for RHEUMATIC PAIN, or, OLD GRIEFS in any PART.

Take of the best Brandy one quart, and Camphire three ounces diffolved in the above Brandy, then add Spirit of Sal Ammoniac two ounces, and Soft Soap eight ounces, mix all together cold in a mortar until thoroughly incorporated, then add Oil of Origanum, and Tincture of Opium, of each four drams, then for ufe. Rub the part afflicted with the above for half an hour together, and rub plenty of the mixture on the part; fhake the bottle well when ufed; and repeat the fame once a-day or as you fee occafion.

The SOAP-EMBROCATION for SOFT SUBSTANCES,

That remain on any joint or part, from the effect of a Bang or Bruife: if the pain is difperfed, take the fediment of Old Sour Lant three half pints, Soft Soap eight ounces, and Oil of Turpentine two ounces, put the whole into a wide-necked large quart bottle, then fhake the bottle, until thoroughly incorporated together, then for ufe. Rub the part afflicted well three times a-day with the above, and obferve to fhake the bottle when ufed; the repetition of the above will fhrink any part flat and fine.

For an OLD PAIN that Remains after LAMENESS in the SHOULDER, KNEE, SINEW, or FETLOCK JOINT.

Take hard Spring Water, and pour it on any of the above parts, out of a garden Watering-pot, and continue fo to do for half an hour together; then wrap the part up warm with Flannel Rollers; repeat the fame every day for a week together. The above application anfwers well to compleat the cure of any old Strains, when no other treatment will.

Section,

Section, 46.

Of BOWEL-GALLS.

IF the above case happens to a Horse on a journey, it generally proceeds as follows: a Horse seldom Bowel-galls if he carries his Girths clear from his Elbows, but if he is pot-bellied he will drive the Girths forward to the Elbows, and most men make a mistake in girthing too tight at them times; or if the above is not the case, it is as follows: some Horses are so fleshy, just out of the Dealer's hands, that their own fat will wrinkle; and is plaited on their Breasts and Chests, much alike unto a plaited shirt, and so heats and galls the parts, but if the complaint proceeds from girthing, make use as follows.

Set the Crupper shorter than common, and let the Girths be very slack and so ride on in that way; and when you come to the Inn, wash the part very clean with warm Table Beer and a Spunge; and when the part is become dry, make use as follows.

A WASH for a BOWEL-GALL.

Take Spirits of Wine two ounces, in a four-ounce bottle, then add to it as much Fuller's Earth as will make it a passable liquid, then for use: rub the part well with the above, and let the Horse only rest one day and two nights, then he will be fit to travel on again.

Alſo for a BOWEL-GALL.

Take a Raw Egg, and dab it gently up to the ſtall-poſt, ſo that you crack the ſhell all around, then take the Egg, Shell and all, and rub the part with it, and repeat the ſame in the morning again, and it will anſwer the purpoſe if you let the Horſe only reſt one day and two nights.

Section, 47.

Of MALLENDERS and SELLANDERS.

THE Mallenders is a hot ſharp humor that breaks out on the bend of the Fore-leg, on the back part of the Knee-joint; and becomes a hot, dry, ſcurfy humor. The Sellanders is on the bend of the Hough on the fore part of the joint: both of the above infirmities make a Horſe very ſtiff and clumſy.

A Valuable OINTMENT for the MALLENDERS.

Take Hogs-lard two ounces, put the above on a Slate, and drop by degrees on the Lard, Oil of Vitriol, and ſo drop more Oil and keep mixing it together with a knife; ſo add more or leſs Oil to the Lard until it comes to a dark grey Ointment, then for uſe; then rub the part once a-day juſt on the ſpot of the Mallenders; rub it well in and it will kill the humor.

The above is a valuable Ointment for a Horſe that hits one Leg againſt the other, and to be made uſe of in the above manner.

Of the MALLENDERS.

For the MALLENDERS.

Take Æthiops Mineral one ounce, white Copperas three drams, and Soft Soap two ounces; mixed cold together for ufe: rub the part well with the above mixture, and rub it in with a green Hazle-ftick, once a-day until the part becomes fcurfy; then give time for the fcurf to come off, of itfelf, then repeat the fame again, in all refpects as above directed.

Alfo for the MALLENDERS.

Take Gunpowder and Glafs made into fine powder, of each one ounce, Oil of Vitriol twenty drops, and Goofe Oil two ounces, all mixed cold together for ufe: then rub the part well as the latter directs in all refpects.

Alfo for the MALLENDERS.

Take the Firing Ointment, fee page 131, and rub the part well with it, and heat it in with a hot iron. The above dreffing will caufe the part to fwell and fweat much; and the part will become fcurfy; when the fcurf comes clear off, repeat the fame again in all refpects.

Both of the above difeafes are alike and are to be cured by the above applications; but in the latter part of the cure, make ufe of the Strong Mercurial Ointment, fee page 68, to rub the part with for fome time, to kill the remaining part of the humor; although fuppofed to be cured, it generally breaks out again as it is a hot humor, that proceeds from the joint.

Section,

Section, 48.

Of SPLENTS and CURBS.

SPLENTS are hard Excrescences on the inside of the Fore-legs, I have oft seen Splents among a stock of young Colts, and seldom saw a yearling Colt but what had Splents more or less, yet the Splents would waste quite away by the time they came to be three years old, with a very little trouble; but if Splents should happen to an old Horse, there must be applications made use of and care taken to reduce them.

As for Curbs, they are a soft oozy relaxation on the hind part of the joint, below the ball of the Hough, and are so common to young Horses, that they will frequently put up a Curb in the time of breaking. A fresh Curb is soon cured if taken in time, and on the other hand, if of old standing, and has been often relaxed it is as obstinate.

For a *Fresh* RELAXED CURB.

Take Spirit of Sal Ammoniac one ounce, Oil of Origanum half an ounce, mixed together; rub the Curb part well with the above once a-day, for a week or nine days, which will reduce any fresh Curb if repeated.

If the above should be applied for a Splent, then add one dram of Euphorbium; but observe to soften the Splent with a Blood-stick first. The above applications are very proper for a fresh Curb or Splent.

For

Of SPLENTS and CURBS.

For SPLENTS or CURBS.

Take Oil of Origanum one ounce and a half, Oil of Turpentine half an ounce, Euphorbium and Cantharides of each one dram, mixed together for use: when used, clip away the hair off the part; then dab and rub the part three times in the space of one hour with the above mixture, then leave of rubbing: the above will cause the part to sweat and scurf much; when the part becomes clear from scurf, repeat the same again in all respects. As for what has been said concerning Splents and Curbs, is of the mildest sorts of applications; and as for old obstinate Splents or Curbs, stronger applications must be made use of as follows.

For Obstinate SPLENTS or CURBS.

Take Spirit of Sal Ammoniac and Egyptiacum of each one ounce, Oil of Origanum one ounce and a half, Cantharides and Euphorbium of each one dram in fine powder, and Sublimate Mercury one dram in fine powder, all mixed together for use; if used for a Splent, first bruise the part with a Bloodstick as before directed; then dab and rub the part afflicted well with the above mixture, three times in the space of one hour. The above will cause a strong scurf to come on the part; give time for the scurf to come off, of itself, then repeat the same again in all respects.

For Obstinate SPLENTS or CURBS.

Take Nerve Ointment one ounce, Spirit of Sal Ammoniac one ounce, and Common Tar one ounce, mixed together, then add, Cantharides and Euphorbium of each two drams and Sublimate Mercury one dram, all made into fine powder, and mixed together for use; if used for a Splent, first bruise it as before directed; then apply on the part, a strong coat of the above mixture with a knife-point: the above will cause a strong scurf to come on the part; then give proper time for the scurf to come off, of itself, then repeat the same again in all respects, as above directed.

The MERCURIAL PLAISTER *for* HARD EXCRESCENCES.

Take Quicksilver two ounces, and Venice Turpentine one ounce; mix and kill the above together in a mortar until the Mercury disappears to the eye; then add strained Galbanum two ounces, Burgundy Pitch three ounces, and Oxycroccum two ounces; melt the three last articles together, and mix them with the above; then add Euphorbium and Cantharides, of each one dram in fine powder: then stir all together, and form the whole into a Roll for use: spread of the above on a Patch of Leather just the size of the Excrescence, and lay it on the part, and confine it on with a Roller. Repeat the same every fortnight or as occasion may require the use of it; and after the use of either of the above applications, and the part is become cool and clear from scurf, if the substance of the Splent or Curb, is not quite reduced flat and fine, then it will be proper to lay the Firing-iron on the part; then apply the Blister after Firing, see page 109, then spread the fired part with the above Blister with a knife, and do not heat it in with a hot iron; then keep his head up for three days and nights; then let him be put into a loose stable for three weeks, then to Grass for three months.

Section,

Section, 49.

****

Of BONE-SPAVINS or RINGBONES.

THE above infirmities are common to Horses of all ages: a Spavin is a hard Excrescence which appears on the inside of the Hough-joint; and the Ringbone is a hard Excrescence on the Instep, sometimes on the Instep of the Fore-foot, and other times on the Instep of the Hind-foot; and both of the above infirmities cause a Horse to be very stiff and lame; particularly at setting out for a journey or elsewhere; although they are both common to Horses, they often proceed from hard work and relaxation of the parts; therefore I would advise, that all moderate and mild applications should be made use of at first, such as mild Blisters and the like; and if a Spavin spreads wide, and seems to be inflamed around the joint, make use of the Mild Blister, see page 108, and apply it all around the joint; and repeat it according as the part requires the use of it; but do not repeat it until the inflammation is quite abated; but if a Spavin is fixed on the usual spot of the joint, make use of the second Blister for a Bone-spavin, see page 111, and repeat it as occasion may require the use of it, but not to be repeated until the inflammation is quite abated.

For SPLENTS, SPAVINS or RINGBONES.

Take Egyptiacum two ounces, Spirit of Sal Ammoniac, Oil of Turpentine and Oil of Origanum of each half an ounce, Oil of Vitriol two drams, all mixed together; then add Euphorbium

phorbium, Cantharides and Sublimate Mercury of each one dram, all mixed together for use; when used, bruise the Spavin or Ringbone with a Blood-stick until they feel soft; then let the above mixture be rubbed well on the part with your finger, and no wider than the substance, and repeat the above dressing for eight mornings together. The above will cause the part to scurf much; then leave of rubbing until the part is clear from scurf, then you may repeat the same again, as above-mentioned.

For a BONE-SPAVIN or RINGBONE.

First clip away the hair off the part; then bruise the Spavin part with a Blood-stick until it feels soft, then rub it with Oil of Origanum twice a-day, and the third day lay on the following Mercurial Plaister.

Take Quicksilver one ounce, and Venice Turpentine half an ounce, mixed and killed together in a mortar, until the Mercury disappears to the eye, then add Burgundy Pitch one ounce, Black Pitch one ounce, and strained Galbanum one ounce; melt the three last articles together, and mix them with the above, then add Cantharides two drams, Euphorbium two drams, and Sublimate Mercury one dram, all in fine powder; then mix the whole together and apply a plaister of it on the part, warm and thick; and bind it on for a fortnight; then repeat the same plaister once again; or you may make use of the Mercurial Plaister, see page 138, which is milder. The last applications are gentle trials and answer sometimes better than stronger mixtures do: but however, if the above do not answer, make use of some of the following applications which are much stronger.

For

Of SPAVINS.

For a BONE-SPAVIN or RINGBONE.

Take White and Yellow Arsenic of each half an ounce in fine powder, Black Soap one ounce and a half, Oil of Vitriol one hundred drops, and Spirit of Lavender one dram, all mixed together for use: then apply the above middling thick on the Spavin part; and as wide as a half-crown piece, and work it in with a knife-point; do not cut away the hair, and in four days time lay on the part, a poultice made of White Bread and Milk, and a little Hogs-lard, and let it remain on one day and night: the above application will turn out a core in about a fortnight's time; then heal it with Tincture of Myrrh, by dabbing the part with the Tincture only.

Also for a BONE-SPAVIN or RINGBONE.

First have the Horse properly cast with hopples; then clip away the hair off the part, then bruise the Spavin or Ringbone with a Blood-stick until it feels soft, then rub it with Oil of Origanum, and rub the Oil well in with your hand on and around the part; then on the Spavin-part just as wide as a half-crown piece, drop three or four drops of Oil of Vitriol, and rub it in with a wooden Splint, and so drop three or four drops more and still rub it in, and so continue until you have dropped and rubbed in twenty drops, but if for a small Spavin, fewer drops may do; when it begins to crack around the sides, anoint the part with Train Oil made hot, then dab it on with a feather, then puff the part with Bole Ammoniac, and so repeat as occasion requires it. The two latter applications will cause a core to come out of any part that they are applied to; then observe to give proper time for the part to cool and heal quite up; then apply the Blistering Charge, see page 112, but if a ſtiffneſs ſhould remain, firſt obſerve to lay the firing-iron on the part, then apply the Bliſter after Firing, ſee page 109, and ſpread it on with a knife, but do not heat it in with a hot iron, and let it remain on as long as poſſible; then tie the Horſe up to the Rack for three days and nights, then let him be turned into a looſe ſtable for three weeks, and then to Graſs for three months at leaſt.

Section, 50.

Of BLOOD or BOG-SPAVINS.

THE Blood-ſpavin is a dilatation or ſwelling of a Vein on the inſide, or hollow of the Hough; or in plain terms where a Vein expands itſelf to a greater bulk than common; and if ſo, the above infirmity will ſoon become an oozy, ſoft, fungous ſubſtance, and will cauſe a Horſe to go very lame; and on the other hand, I have known the above infirmity to proceed from their parentage, either from the Horſe or the Mare, or both of them; therefore, I would adviſe that no Gentlemen will breed out of ſuch as them.

To Eaſe a BLOOD-SPAVIN for the preſent Time.

Take the Gall-embrocation, ſee page 127, and rub the part well with it; and it will give eaſe, until ſuch time you have an opportunity to take up the Veins; then proceed as follows.

For a BLOOD-SPAVIN.

In the firſt place, let the Vein be taken up by ſome ſkilful hand, above and below the Hough-joint; then bathe the Spavin part only, with the following mixture.

Take

Of BLOOD SPAVINS.

Take Old Verjuice and Oak Bark, and boil them together, then add Bole Ammoniac two ounces to every quart of Verjuice and Bark; then bathe the part with the above, cold, twice a-day, and so continue bathing all the time, whilst the wounds where the Veins were taken up are a healing; then if the part is quite reduced, lay the firing-iron on, and make use of the Blister after Firing, on the part, see page 109; on the other hand, if the part is not quite reduced flat, and the substance should remain, then make use of the Vitriol Blister, see page 109, and repeat the Blister two or three times; but do not repeat it until the scurf is clear off the part; then lay the firing-iron on, and observe to draw your lines with the iron about three parts of an inch distant from each other, and just as deep as the pressure of the iron causes the part or scores to look quite yellow; then apply the Blister after Firing on the part, and at the same time make use of a loose stable for three weeks, then turn him to Grass for two months or longer.

But if a Blood-spavin or Thorough-pin on the Hough part, should prove obstinate, make use of the Blister for a Let-down Sinew, see page 109, observing the precautions there given, in all respects.

For a SINUS on the HOUGH.

Take strong Spirits of Wine four ounces, Camphire one ounce, Spirit of Sal Ammoniac two ounces, the Extract of Saturn two ounces, mixed together; rub the Sinus well twice a-day. The above if repeated will shrink any Sinus on the Hough or elsewhere.

Section, 51.

Of STRAINS in the BACK SINEWS.

THE above accidents are common; and all men that have had the least practice among Horses, must without a doubt, be well acquainted with the symptoms thereof; therefore, there is no need of further explanation; but so far, I would advise that all fresh Sinew-strains should be treated, at first, with mild applications; and so continue until the inflammation is quite abated; as so, proceed as follows.

In the first place take blood from the Spurn-vein in the toe; catch the blood, and add to it a handful of Common Salt, then bathe the Sinew well with the Blood and Salt; the next morning make use of the following mixture.

An EMBROCATION for a Fresh STRAIN in the SINEWS.

Take Strong Verjuice one pint, Spirits of Wine half a pint, Camphire one ounce, dissolved in the Spirits, Spirits of Hartshorn one ounce, Bole Ammoniac three ounces, all mixed together; rub the part once a-day and bind it up with a Flannel Roller. The following account is but simple, but ought not to be omitted, as it is valuable.

For a Fresh STRAIN in the SINEWS.

Take a Hay-rope or Band and wet it well in hard Spring Water; then bind it around the Leg close; then pour Spring Water on the Hay-band and Sinew, three or four times a-day, and repeat it for six days together, observing not to stir the Horse

Of STRAINS in the BACK SINEWS.

Horfe out all the time; the repetition of the above, if a frefh Strain generally promotes a cure.

The SHAVINGS-POULTICE for a FRESH STRAIN in the SINEWS.

Take ftrong Verjuice one quart; and dry Currier's Shavings, a fufficient quantity to make the whole into a Poultice, by boiling them together over a flow fire, to the confiftence of a Poultice; then apply it to the part, and repeat it in three days, or as occafion may require the ufe of it.

For a Frefh STRAIN in the BACK-SINEWS, or for any Soft Subftance on the KNEE or FETLOCK-JOINT, or to Suck a THORN out of any Part.

Take Soft Soap two pounds, Bole Ammoniac in powder two ounces, then add Spirits of Wine fix ounces, Camphire in powder one ounce, Spirit of Sal Ammoniac one ounce, Spirits of Hartfhorn one ounce, all mixed together in a mortar and kept in a clofe covered pot for ufe; and when ufed, rub any of the above parts well, and fpread a pledget of Tow, with the above application and bind it on the part with a Flannel Roller, and repeat the above every third day. The above application if continued for fome time, will reduce any part fine and firm.

What has been faid concerning Strains in the Sinews, are fufficient to cure any frefh Strains in the above parts, and will anfwer at firft better than ftronger applications; but if the Sinews are broken down and badly relaxed, and feels hard and callous, proceed as follows. Take the Soap and Brandy Charge, and rub it well on, and heat it in with a hot iron.

The *SOAP* and *BRANDY CHARGE.*

The Charge is made by boiling Soft Soap four ounces, and Brandy half a pint, to the confiftence of a Charge over a flow fire. The above application will caufe the part to fwell much, but the fwelling will foon drop flat again: repeat the fame again in all refpects for three or four times, but not to be repeated until you fee the Sinew clear from fcurf and the inflammation quite abated.

For an *OLD STRAIN* in the *BACK SINEWS.*

Take Spirits of Wine ftrongly camphorated four ounces, and Cantharides in fine powder two ounces, mixed together for ufe: when ufed, add to one ounce of the above mixture, one ounce of Brandy; then rub the Sinew well with the above mixture, it will caufe the Sinew to fwell and fweat much: when the inflammation is abated, and the Sinew is clear from fcurf, repeat the fame again in all refpects, for three or four dreffings.

For an *Obftinate STRAIN* in the *SINEWS.*

Take the Firing Ointment, fee page 131, and rub the Sinew well with it, then heat it in with a hot iron. The above will caufe the Sinew to fwell and fweat much; then obferve to give time for the inflammation to abate and the fcurf to come off, of itfelf; then repeat the fame again in all refpects for three or four dreffings, or as you fee the part require.

For an *Obftinate STRAIN* in the *SINEWS.*

Take the Black Oils, fee page 130, and make ufe of them, as the latter directs you in all refpects. The above Oils feldom fail to perform a cure of a broken-down Sinew, if repeated as the latter.

Of STRAINS in the BACK SINEWS.

For obstinate Strains of Sinews, I have recommended the four last applications, which are very strong, and much of the blistering kind; and I shall only add one more of the kind, which is as follows.

Take the Strong Blister for a let-down Sinew, see page 110, and rub the Sinew well with it, and observe not to heat it in with a hot iron. The above will swell and sweat the Sinew much; then give proper time for the scurf to come off, of itself, then repeat the same again in all respects for three or four dressings; after the last dressing, with any of the above applications and the Sinew is become fine and firm, and the scurf clear off, then it would be proper to lay the firing-iron on the Sinew; then apply the Blister after Firing, see page 109, on the part, but do not heat it in with a hot iron; then tie his head up for four days and nights, then turn him into a loose stable for a month, and then to Grass for four months at least. The above method always served my purpose.

To RELAX any CONTRACTED SINEW.

Take Clarified Marrow from Deers shanks half a pint, and Old Rum half a pint, mixed together cold in a quart bottle for use; shake the mixture well when used, and rub the Sinew well with it, and heat it in with a hot iron. Repeat the same twice a-day, and keep the part warm with Flannel Rollers.

Also to RELAX a CONTRACTED SINEW.

Take Spent Oil and rub any contracted part with the above Oil, and let it be rubbed well in once a-day, which will relax any contracted part. The above Oil is to be had of some of the noted Skinners.

Section,

Section, 52.

Of STRAINS in the PASTERN or COFFIN-JOINT.

IF fresh Strains in either of the above parts; first bleed in the Spurn-vein of the Foot; then take Black Soap two ounces, Brandy one gill, and Oil of Turpentine one ounce, Spirits of Sal Ammoniac one ounce, mixed together; then rub the part well with the above, and lap it up with a Flannel Roller; and repeat the same once a-day, or as occasion may require the use of it.

A POULTICE for the PASTERN or COFFIN-JOINT.

Take Camomile, Wormwood, Foxglove, and Hemlock, of each a full handful pounded green in a mortar together; then add strong Verjuice one pint, and the grounds of old Lant one pint; put the whole into a saucepan over a slow fire, then make it into a Poultice with Malt ground fine, then for use; then apply the above Poultice warm to the part, and repeat the same once a-day, or as occasion may require the use of it. The above is a valuable Poultice if continued.

If the above LAMENESS should prove Obstinate,

Take Butterton's Water, see page 129, and rub the part well with it once a-day, until the part becomes scurfy and sweats much; then leave off rubbing until the part becomes cool and clear from scurf; then repeat the same again, in all respects as above-directed.

A BLISTER

Of STRAINS in the PASTERN or COFFIN.

A BLISTER for an Obstinate STRAIN in the PASTERN or COFFIN-JOINT.

Take the Strong Blistering Ointment for a let-down Sinew, see page 109, rub either of the above parts with the Ointment, and rub it in well with your hand; then observe to give time for the part to cool and become clear from scurf before you repeat the second Blister.

After the above methods have been made use of, and the part is become fine and firm, then it will be proper to lay the firing-iron on the part; then apply the Blister after Firing, see page 109, on the part, and not to be heated in with a hot iron.

When you fire either the Pastern or Coffin-joint, you must observe that the skin is thicker in that part than in any other part of the body, except the Whirlbone, therefore you must fire the Pastern or Coffin deeper than any other part of the body, except the Whirlbone. On the other hand, I have known several Horses lame in the Nut or Coffin-bone, to which the best of applications were made use of, but all to no purpose; as I have been an eye-witness to several Horses lame in the Coffin-bone, and in those days I thought myself in the wrong, as I could not compleat a cure on them; but since then I stuck a Horse which was lame in the Nut-bone which resteth upon the Coffin, broke in three pieces; and since then I have seen several of the same kind; and if the case should prove so, there is no hope of a cure; therefore rest content with the loss of your Horse, and so-forth.

Section, 53.

Of FRACTURES or BROKEN BONES.

IF a Fracture fhould happen, and the Bone is badly fhattered and bolted through the Skin, it is of no ufe to attempt to fet it; as a Horfe's Leg or Thigh muft be tied up tight; and not like unto a Man's Leg that has a compound Fracture, who is kept ftill in bed and may have the Wounds dreffed every day; but when a Horfe's Leg or Thigh is fet, it muft take its chance, and is not to be opened for two months at leaft: and if a compound Fracture that is badly fhattered, fhould be fet and tied up, it is certain to mortify, for want of being opened and the wounds dreffed: but if the fkin is whole, and the Bone is not ftarted through the fkin, you may fet the Leg or Thigh as follows.

Take a quart of Verjuice and fix Eggs, both Whites and Yolks and Bole Ammoniac four ounces, mix and beat them well together; then take two Linen Rollers, each three yards in length, and dip and foak them in the above mixture; then ftraighten the Leg or Thigh, and fet the Fracture, then roll the above Rollers around the part tolerable tight; then obferve to lay on the Rollers a piece of Pafteboard dipped in the aforefaid mixture, to fit the Leg like the Bark to a Tree; then roll on the Pafteboard a light Roller to keep it on; then prepare as many wooden Splints as will keep the Leg firm and ftraight; then take a long Roller dipped and foaked in a Batter, made of Verjuice and the Whites of four Eggs and Wheat Flour, and roll it around upon the Splints; then keep the

Horfe

Of GRAPY HEELS.

Horfe ftill until the cement is dried and fixed, then let him be in a loofe ftable, and in two months time take the Rollers and Bandages off, and apply the Strengthening Charge, fee page 113, bind it up with a piece of Pafteboard and a Roller, and let it remain on for two months at leaft; the above method always ferved my purpofe.

Section, 54.

Of GRAPY HEELS.

THE Grapes are filthy, ftinking, growing bunches, refembling Warts, which grow upon Horfes Heels and Fetlock-joints, and are own coufins to the inveterate Greafe, which has been ill cured by the ufe of drying applications, and badly treated by drying up the humor too quick, and that generally caufes thick gummy Legs and the like. Alfo make ufe as follows.

A PLAISTER for GRAPY HEELS.

Take White Mercury in fine powder one ounce, and Ointment of Marfh Mallows five ounces, mixed together for ufe; then fpread of the above on pledgets of Tow, and apply it on the part, and bind it clofe to, for fix days; then obferve to renew the Plaifter, and fo continue every fix days until the part is become flat and fine, and all the fpungy Grapes quite fluffed clear off the the part: then heal it with Egyptiacum, fee page 90, or make ufe of the ftrong drying and healing mixture for the Inveterate Greafe, fee page 154, and make ufe of it as it is there recommended, in every refpect; and at the

fame

same time, give two or three Piffing Drinks, fee page 27, then give the Strong Drink for an Inveterate Farcy, fee page 72; give three or four of the above drinks, one to be given every fourth day; and obferve to keep the Horfe in a loofe ftable during all the time of the cure.

Section, 55.

Of the GREASE.

MOST Horfes are fubject to the Greafe; the caufe of it is hard labour and bad management after, infomuch that the Legs and Limbs will fwell and become fhort of action, and due circulation; then foon will come to be the rank Greafe, if not taken in time; and if not broken out, make ufe as follows. Firft make ufe of a loofe ftable, then bleed, and give fome of the Piffing Balls, fee page 26, and make ufe of fome mild fomentation to the Legs; and after each fomenting, rub the part well with Spirits of Wine and Camphire, then wrap the Leg up warm with Flannel Rollers; but if broken out, make ufe of the following Poultice.

A POULTICE for the GREASE.

Take Green Cabbage-leaves a double handful, and one large Onion, and pound them fmall in a mortar; then add Grounds of Old Beer one pint; make the above hot together in a fauce-pan, then add Hogs-lard two ounces, and Horfe Turpentine one ounce; make the whole into the confiftence of a Poultice with Rye Flour, or Bran; and repeat the fame every day, to the Heels.

A Stronger

Of the GREASE.

A Stronger POULTICE for the GREASE.

Take three Heads of Garlic, and four moderate fized Onions, bruifed together in a mortar; then add Grounds of Beer one pint, make the above hot together in a faucepan; then add Hogs-lard four ounces, Honey two meat-fpoonfuls, and Horfe Turpentine two ounces; and make the whole into the confiftence of a Poultice, with Rye Flour, or Bran, then for ufe. The above to be repeated as occafion may require the ufe of it. When ufed, clip away the hair, then apply either of the above Poultices to the part, and repeat it for five or fix days together: the above Poultices will fuck the humor and venom out of the part: then make ufe of the following healing and drying Plaifter.

The HEALING PLAISTER for the GREASE.

Take Hogs-lard fix ounces, and the Lees of Red-wine one pound, firft mix the above together, then add Honey and Horfe Turpentine of each half a pound, and melt the whole together over a flow fire, then add Roch-allum in fine powder one ounce and a half, and Egg-fhells in fine powder two ounces, ftir the above all together until quite cold, then for ufe; then wafh the part with Soap and Water, when dry, apply the above Plaifter, fpread upon a pledget of Tow, on the part, and bind it clofe on.

Repeat the above Plaifter every other day; two or three of the above Plaifters will promote a cure.

If the above Plaifter fhould not prove ftrong enough, make ufe of the following mixture.

The DRYING and HEALING MIXTURE for an INVETERATE GREASE.

Take Verjuice one quart, drop into it Oil of Vitriol one ounce, and mix them together; then take Red Precipitate half an ounce, and Egyptiacum six ounces; mix the two laſt articles together in a mortar, then add to the above, Tincture of Myrrh with Aloes four ounces; then mix all together, and put the whole into a large quart bottle for uſe; when uſed, ſhake the mixture well and dip a pledget of Tow in the above mixture, and dab and waſh the part twice a-day: the above will heal and dry up moſt ſharp humors whatever; the above is a very ſtrong aſtringent, and might be made uſe of, if the Healing Plaiſter fails; and at the ſame time give a few Piſſing Balls, ſee page 27, according as they operate; then a doſe or two of purging phyſic will be proper to be made uſe of.

Section, 56.

Of HEEL-OINTMENTS.

THE following Ointments, are cooling, and healing to the Heels; and are proper to rub a little into the Heels at night, eſpecially after a journey when the roads are dry and hard; and alſo, are uſeful for Horſes that are in training, as they are often obliged to take their exerciſe on hard ground, eſpecially in dry ſummers; and when the ground is hard the Heels are ſubject to crack and tear; and more ſo in ſome Horſes than others.

Of HEEL-OINTMENTS.

The HEEL-OINTMENT.

Take Deers Suet four ounces, Bees-wax two ounces, Sweet Oil half a pint, and Lapis Calaminaris two ounces in fine powder, all melted together over a flow fire, and then ſtirred until almoſt cold; then add Camphire four drams diſſolved in a little Spirits of Wine, then ſtirred all together until quite cold, then for uſe. The above is a good Cerate.

A COOLING HEALING EMBROCATION for the HEELS.

Take Spirits of Wine two ounces, diſſolve therein as much Camphire as the Spirits will diſſolve, the Extract of Saturn one ounce and a half, Sweet Oil ſix ounces, mix all together in a bottle for uſe; and when the Legs are clean and dry, ſhake the mixture well, then apply ſome of the above mixture to the Heels with your fingers at any time; the above is very cooling and healing, to torn and ſcratched Heels and Legs, after a hard day's hunting or the like.

The COMMON HEEL-OINTMENT.

Take Plantane Leaves, Allheal and Primroſe Leaves of each a full handful, bruiſe the above in a mortar; then add Mutton Suet and Train Oil of each one pound; melt and ſlew the above all together over a flow fire, then ſtrain it for uſe, then put the above Ointment into a pot, and ſtir it until quite cold. The above is a good Common Heel-ointment, and may be made uſe of as the latter Ointments are recommended in all reſpects; when a Horſe is dreſſed up clean and dry, rub ſome of the above Ointment into the Heels, and it will keep them mellow and ſupple.

For

Of a CANCEROUS HUMOR.

For HORSES HEELS that are Burnt in the Lime.

Take Common Linseed Oil one pint, Sugar of Lead five ounces, diffolved in five ounces of the beft ftrong Vinegar, Spirits of Wine three ounces, Camphire one ounce diffolved in the above Spirits, all mixed together in a mortar, then for ufe; then dab and fmear the Heels at a night, after they have been wafhed clean and is become dry.

Section, 57.

Of a CANCEROUS HUMOR on the LEGS and HEELS.

THE above is a fharp, rafh Humor, that fpreads from the Knee downwards all along the Legs, of a thick hard dry fcurf; and as the above diforder is not common, neither did I fee any of the above diforder, but very feldom in this neighbourhood; I have brought feveral lots of young Horfes from Yorkfhire, and to the beft of my memory I never brought any from that quarter, but what had more or lefs of the above diforder; therefore I thought it proper to mention it here; as fo, make ufe of the following Ointment.

The OINTMENT for the above.

Take the Herb Hemlock, the deadly Night Shade, Plantane, Allheal, Primrofe Leaves, Dwarf Elder, Groundfel, Crowfoot, and the fharp-pointed Dock-root, of each a full handful, all bruifed together in a mortar; then fimmer the whole over a flow fire, with five pounds of Frefh Butter without Salt, for an hour together; then ftrain and prefs the Ointment out for ufe;

use; rub the parts afflicted once a-day with the above Ointment; I could not manage the above diforder until I contrived the above Ointment. They say in Yorkshire, that the above diforder proceeds from a venomous herb, that grows in their pastures. The above Ointment, being made use of, as above directed, will kill the humor, and heal and clear the scurf off the part.

Section, 58.

Of QUITTER BONES.

THE above is an Ulcer, or Cavity, larger or lesser according to the size of the Quitter; full of Ulcers like unto a Rabbit's burrow; the general cause thereof, is an accident, or a violent crush, stab, or wound of some kind on the coronet part of the Foot, sometimes on the inside, and sometimes on the outside of the Foot; and if a fresh crush or stab on the coronet, and the part is become a spungy soft substance, which commonly is the case; and if so, make use of the following Sucking Plaister.

Take Soft Soap and Common Salt of each the same quantity, mixed together in a mortar for use. Apply a thick Plaister of the above on the part; and repeat four or five of the above Plaisters, one every other day; the repetition of the above will burst the part open, and suck the venom out; but sometimes in the first dressing, I add to the above Plaister a very little Quicklime, in powder, when I mean to make it stronger, in order to throw out a core; then make use of the following mixture to heal it.

Of QUITTER-BONES.

The MILD QUITTER OILS.

Take Spirits of Wine, one ounce, Oil of Turpentine one ounce, Egyptiacum one ounce; Red Precipitate one dram, and Aquafortis half an ounce, Oil of Vitriol two drams; first mix the Egyptiacum and the Precipitate together in a mortar; then add the others and mix them all together for use; and when used after the above Plaister; dip a pledget of Tow in the mixture, and dab the part and tie the said pledget to the wound; and repeat the same once a-day; the above will heal the part firm; and if the above fails a cure, make use of the Strong Quitter Oils, as follows.

The STRONG QUITTER OILS.

Take Egyptiacum two ounces, Red Precipitate two drams; first mix the above together in a mortar; then add Spirits of Wine, Oil of Turpentine, Oil of Origanum, and Oil of Petre, of each one ounce; then add to the above by degrees, Oil of Vitriol, and Double Aquafortis, of each six drams, all mixed carefully together in a mortar for use; and when used, shake the mixture well, then let the above be rubbed and dabbed on the part for eight mornings together. If the above application should dry the part too quick, leave of rubbing, then the above will prove a cure, and if not, make use of the following method.

For a LARGE QUITTER-BONE.

If the Quitter seems in a dangerous way, first unsole the Foot; but if a moderate sized Quitter you need not take the sole out, but observe to pare and dress the Foot underneath very thin, then take the horn or husk-part of the Foot away, opposite the tread of the Quitter, so that the shoe doth not

rest

Of QUITTER-BONES.

rest on the Foot-part oppofite the Quitter; then fet on a Barfhoe, and proceed as follows.

First clip away the hair off the part, then take a ftiff blunt Butcher's fkewer, and thruft it into the bottom of every fountain of the Quitter, fo that you provoke the ulcer or wound to bleed much; then lay in each fountain a fmall Tent of Tow dipped in Double Aquafortis, then fet the Foot down to the ground for two or three minutes, then draw out the Tents; then fet in frefh Tents dipped in the fame, which are to remain in; then obferve to rub on, and around the part a little Oil of Turpentine, then rub on a very little Aquafortis, and fo continue rubbing firft the one, and then the other, for five or feven times each, according to the fize of the Quitter; beginning with the Oil of Turpentine and end with the Aquafortis; then heat the Quitter-part with a hot flat-iron at a proper diftance, until the Quitter feems to turn yellow. Keep the Horfe in for a-day and a-night; and then turn him to Grafs; and in four days time fcald the part with equal quantities of Black Pitch, Tar and Tallow, made quite fcalding hot together, then immediately poured into the wound out of a ladle; and repeat the fcalding three or four times, once every other day. The above method properly obferved will cure moft Quitters whatever; do not fuffer the wound to be dreffed with no other application. The above feldom fails a cure if properly obferved. It never failed me on the above occafion.

For an Obftinate PETRIFIED QUITTER-BONE, that has been badly Managed.

Firft unfole the Foot, then drefs and pare the Foot as I have directed in the latter; then clip away the hair off the part,
then

then fire the Quitter, after the following form or figure, fire the Half-moon figure almost through the skin, and the specks within the circle must be burned quite through the skin with an iron much the shape of a tobacco-pipe's shank, then put into each hole the size of a small pea of Sublimate Mercury, wrapped in Soft Paper; then cover the part with Black Pitch and a very little Tallow made warm together, and laid on in the form of a Charge; bind it close to the part for four days; then cut the ties or bandages off, and let the Charge drop off, of itself; when the part is cracked around, and the core is almost out, scald the part with equal parts of Black Pitch, Tar, and Tallow, made quite scalding hot together, and immediately poured into the wound; the above scalding to be repeated twice a-week. The above method properly observed will promote a cure.

To Destroy an ULCER that Remains in a QUITTER-BONE.

Take Oil of Vitriol two drams, Sublimate Mercury in fine powder one dram, mixed together in a small wide-mouthed bottle for use; and when used, shake the above well together, then take a blunt Butcher's skewer and wrap the end round with Tow, then dip it in the above mixture, and thrust it into the bottom of the Ulcer, and trace the Ulcer round within-side. The above will destroy any Ulcer. The above application is not to be repeated for nine days to come; the above dressing will cause the part to discharge much.

Section,

Section, 59.

Of OVER-REACHES or FRESH STABS on the CORONET-PART of the FOOT.

OVER-REACHES are a catch from the Hind-toe to the Cap of the Heel of the Fore-foot, so bad at sometimes that the Cap of the Fore-heel is quite sheared off, by the tread of the Hind-toe; and if fresh, make use as follows, first observing to cut the flap off the part.

For a FRESH OVER-REACH.

Take Spirits of Wine and Oil of Turpentine of each one pint, and Colcothar of Vitriol four ounces in very fine powder, all mixed together for use; when used, dip a pledget of Tow in the above mixture, and dab the part well with it; then bind the said pledget to the wound, and repeat the same twice a-day; and let the Horse stand in for six or eight days; the use of the above will cement and heal the part firm, if applied as above-mentioned. Observe to shake the mixture well when used.

Also for an OVER-REACH.

Take Verjuice one quart; drop into it Oil of Vitriol one ounce, mix the above first together, then add Red Precipitate six drams, and Egyptiacum four ounces; mix the two last articles well together in a mortar, then add Tincture of Myrrh with Aloes four ounces, then mix the whole together for use; shake the bottle well when used; then dip a pledget of Tow in the above mixture and dab the part, then bind the said pledget to the part; repeat the above twice a-day, and keep the Horse in for five or six days.

For an Old OVER-REACH, STAB, or TREAD, on the CORONET-PART, that is ULCERATED.

In the firſt place dip a ſmall pledget of Tow in Butter of Antimony; then thruſt the pledget into the bottom of the Ulcer with a Probe, then directly take it out, and put a freſh pledget of the ſame in, and there let it remain; then immediately apply the following Sucking Plaiſter.

Take Soft Soap and Common Salt, of each the ſame quantity mixed together in a mortar to a Plaiſter; repeat five or ſix of the above Plaiſters, one every other day; and when the Ulcer is clear at the bottom, make uſe of the following mixture.

Take Egyptiacum three ounces, and Red Precipitate three drams, mixed together in a mortar; then add Spirits of Wine, Oil of Turpentine, and Aquafortis, of each one ounce, and mix the whole together for uſe; when uſed ſhake the bottle well, and dab the part once a-day, with a pledget of Tow dipped in the above mixture; then bind the ſaid pledget to the part; obſerve to keep the Horſe in a looſe ſtable during the time of the cure.

Section, 60.

Of SAND-CRACKS.

SAND-CRACKS, are ſmall Cracks on the inſide of the Foot, and ſometimes on the outſide of the Foot; and commonly crack downwards, through the Coronet-part, halfway down to the ſhoe; but moſt commonly happen on the inſide of the Foot; rather nearer to the Heel-part. The above generally happen to narrow wire-heeled Horſes; alſo, there is another ſort

Of SAND-CRACKS.

fort of Sand-cracks, that appears on the fore-part of the Foot, and cracks down from the Inftep-part of the Coronet to the Toe; and is very wide, much like unto a Cow's claw; and both make a Horfe very lame. I have known Horfes to fplit of Sand-cracks, in running a heat, or by fweating upon hard ground, that you might have tracked them by their own blood; which made them unfit for bufinefs for fome time; alfo hacks that travel upon hard dry roads, are equally fubject to the above cafe; therefore make ufe of the following methods; firft, pare and drefs the Foot, underneath the tread of the Sand-crack, with a fharp drawing-knife and rafp, and cut away the lips or edges of the Sand-crack, then fet on a barfhoe; and always obferve that the hufk or horn of the Foot is taken away, oppofite the tread of the Sand-crack, fo that the fhoe doth not reft on, nor nigh that part; then on the Coronet-part acrofs the top of the Sand-crack, make three fcores with the firing-iron. Then make ufe of the following mixture.

A MIXTURE for a SAND-CRACK.

Take Spirits of Wine and Oil of Turpentine, of each one pint, and Colcothar of Vitriol in fine powder four ounces, all mixed together for ufe; then dab the Sand-crack with a pledget of Tow dipped in the above mixture, and bind the faid pledget to the part; the above will kill and heal the Sand-crack. On the other hand, if the Vein fhould happen to puff up in the flit of the Sand-crack, make ufe of the following mixture.

Take Tincture of Myrrh with Aloes one ounce, and Aquafortis half an ounce, mixed together for ufe; and to be ufed in all refpects as the latter directs you; or if the Sand-crack is of an old ftanding, and is hollow and ulcerated, pare the Foot as I have before directed, and fet on a bar-fhoe; then make ufe of the following mixture.

A MIXTURE for an ULCERATED SAND-CRACK.

Take Egyptiacum three ounces, and Red Precipitate three drams, mix the above together in a mortar, then add Spirits of Wine one ounce, Oil of Turpentine one ounce, and double Aquafortis one ounce, Oil of Vitriol two drams, all mixed together for ufe; dab the part once a-day with a pledget of Tow dipped in the above mixture, and bind the faid pledget to the part, and fo continue, until the Sand-crack is killed, and begins to unite together at the Coronet-part; at the fame time make ufe of a loofe ftable, then make ufe of the following healing Plaifter.

A HEALING PLAISTER for a SAND-CRACK.

Take Black Pitch and Bees-wax of each five ounces, Common Tar, and Tallow of each one ounce, all melted together over a flow fire; then add Bole Ammoniac four ounces in fine powder, and ftir the whole together until quite cold, then for ufe; fpread fome of the above on a pledget of Tow, and bind it clofe to the part; and repeat the fame twice a-week; the above will heal the Sand-crack up firm. But if a Sand-crack happens on the Inftep-part like unto a Cow's claw, you muft open it as before directed; and obferve to pare the hufk of the Toe as fhort as you poffibly can; then draw a deep groove, quite acrofs the Sand-crack juft below the Coronet, with a drawing-knife, quite to the quick; then fet on a bar-fhoe; and obferve to treat the above, as I have mentioned before, in every refpect concerning a Sand-crack on the fide of the Foot.

Section,

Section, 61.

****

Of RUNNING THRUSHES in the FROG of the FOOT.

THE above is a rotten, feeding, stinking, sharp Humor, or rather a cancerous Ulcer, that some Horses are very subject to, that have narrow and steep Heels, and commonly are soft and ragged in the Frog-part; which make a Horse go tender and lame. Nor is it proper to dry the Humor up at all times, for I have seen Horses that had Thrushes in the Feet, which had been dried up too quick, and so the Humor returned up into the Eyes, and the Horse thereby became blind. As so, make use of the following safe method at first for a trial.

First of all cut and pare the rotten part of the Frog away; then thin the sole of the Foot round the borders of the Frog; then wash and dab the Foot withinside and outside, three times a-day with Old Lant warmed with a hot iron. The above application always served my purpose; and observe at the same time to give a course of Pissing Balls, see page 27. But if the above should prove obstinate, you may make use as follows. If the Frog should prove more spungy than common, take Roman Vitriol two ounces, in very fine powder, Bole Ammoniac one ounce, in fine powder, mixed well together; then pare the rotten part of the Frog away; then sprinkle the above powder on the part, and smear it on with your finger; then stop the Foot up with dry Tow. Repeat the above every other day. The above application will dry the part up, at the same time observe to give Pissing Balls for some time, or

Q q take

take Egyptiacum three ounces, and Red Precipitate three drams, and mix them well together in a mortar; then add Spirits of Wine and Oil of Turpentine of each one ounce, and Aquafortis one ounce, all mixed together for ufe; dip a fmall pledget of Tow in the above mixture, and apply it on the part; obferve to fhake the bottle when ufed; repeat the fame once a-day, and at the fame time make ufe of the following mixture.

A Drying MIXTURE for a Running THRUSH.

Take Common Tar one pint, and Common Allum in fine powder three ounces, mixed together cold for ufe: fpread a plaifter of the above, upon Tow, and apply it to the part, and cover it up with dry Tow; repeat the drefling every other day; alfo, I will advife that all Horfes that are kept in the ftable, if they are fubject to Thrufhes; fhould have their Feet well wafhed, within and without, three times a-day with Old Lant kept in readinefs for that purpofe; and never greafe a Horfe's Foot, but after a hard journey, and no other time, for greafe is hurtful to the Feet of fuch Horfes.

Section, 62.

Of WOUNDS in General in the FEET.

THE Feet are liable to be wounded from feveral weapons, fuch as Nails, broken Glafs-bottles, Stubs, Thorns, or the like weapons. If a Foot fhould be wounded from any of the above weapons, firft obferve to open the part with a drawing-knife to the bottom, and be careful to take all the offender out; and if a Nail or any other weapon has wounded

or

Of WOUNDS in the FEET.

or injured the Coffin-bone, it muſt be opened to the Coffin, with an iron made in the half-moon form, like unto a Gouge-chiſel; and with the ſaid iron made quite hot, take as wide as a half-crown piece of the fleſhy part away that lieth between the Sole-part and the Coffin-bone; in order for an Exfoliation of the Bone, before any attempts of a cure; and as for the treatment of the above, I will endeavour to ſet all down ſeparately, with the method of unſoling the Foot, and how to treat the ſame in every reſpect, as follows.

For a STAB of a NAIL on the ROAD by an ACCIDENT.

If but a ſlight Wound, make uſe of the following mixture; firſt open the part a very little with a drawing-knife; then take Tincture of Myrrh with Aloes one ounce, and Aquafortis half an ounce mixed together for uſe; dab the part ſparingly; then taper it with a hammer, to cauſe the mixture to penetrate into the Wound. The above method always anſwered my purpoſe, when, at the ſame time, I had a long journey to go.

For a SEVERE WOUND in the FOOT.

Where the Coffin is ſafe, and not injured, firſt open the part to the quick; then take a ſmall pledget of Tow dipped in Oil of Turpentine, and dab the Wound; then apply the ſaid pledget on the Wound, and lay upon that, another thick pledget of dry Tow; then on the dry pledget apply one ounce of the Digeſtive Green Ointment, ſee page 82, then heat the Ointment quite through the pledget, down to the bottom of the Wound with a hot iron of the let-iron kind, the form of which is like a poker with a flat blunt nozle: repeat the dreſſing every other day; and at the ſame time make uſe

of

of the following hot Stopping if occasion may require the use of it, and the pain continues great.

The HOT STOPPING.

Take Common Tar, Tallow and Horse Turpentine, of each the same quantity, made hot together in a ladle, and made into the consistence of a poultice with Wheat Bran. The Foot may be stopped up with the above after every dressing, if occasion may require; after the use of the above method, and the Wound begins to incarnate, and the pain is abated, make use of the following mixture to heal the part up.

The HEALING FOOT-MIXTURE.

Take Egyptiacum one ounce, and Red Precipitate one dram, mix the above together in a mortar; then add Spirits of Wine and Oil of Turpentine of each one ounce and Aquafortis half an ounce, all mixed together for use; dip a pledget of Tow in the above mixture and apply it on the Wound; repeat the same every other day, or as occasion may require the use of it.

For the COFFIN-BONE, when WOUNDED by an ACCIDENT with a NAIL.

First observe to open the part with the iron, as I have before directed; then treat the Wound as follows.

Take Tincture of Myrrh with Aloes one ounce, Strong Ticture of Euphorbium half an ounce, and Oil of Turpentine two drams, mixed together for use; dab the Wound with a pledget of Tow dipped in the above mixture, and apply the said pledget on the wounded Bone; then lay a thick pledget of dry Tow on the other pledget, and lay one ounce of the

Digestive

Of WOUNDS in the FEET.

Digeſtive Green Ointment upon that, ſee page 82, then heat it well into the bottom of the Wound with a hot iron; and continue the above dreſſing until the Bone is exfoliated clear off the part; and ſtop the Foot up with the aforeſaid Hot Stopping if occaſion be; repeat the dreſſings every other day, and if the pain ſhould continue great, make uſe of the following Poultice.

Take Old Lant made into the conſiſtence of a Poultice with Wheat Bran and a very little Hogs-lard; apply the Poultice around the Foot, on a Cloth, and tie it up with a Liſt around the Paſtern; repeat the above Poultice once a-day, or as occaſion may require the uſe of it; and if a ſevere humor ſhould attend the Foot, you muſt unſole it, and then proceed as follows.

The METHOD of UNSOLING the FOOT.

Firſt pare the Foot underneath with a Butteris; then the pith will appear, between the ſole and the huſk as Nature ordained it: then take a drawing-knife and draw a groove around the Foot, and follow the pith all around from Heel to Heel; obſerve to draw the groove quite to the quick, and be ſure to looſen the Heel-parts well; then preſs with your thumb on the groove or drawn-part, then you will find whether it is ſufficiently weakened between the huſk and the ſole, and if you find the part quite at the quick, tie a Liſt tight about the Paſtern to ſtagnate the blood; then with a ſharp penknife divide the ſole from the huſk, then prize up the edge of the ſole quite around with a prizing-chiſel; then lug the ſole off gradually with the aſſiſtance of a pair of pincers; then untie the Liſt and let the Foot bleed plentifully; then dreſs the Foot up as follows.

Of WOUNDS in the FEET.

First dab the sole-part with Oil of Turpentine; then set on the shoe with a piece of Leather underneath it, the whole width of the Foot; then stop the Foot up underneath the Leather with Tow dipped in Oil of Turpentine; repeat the above dressing three times, once every other day; then make use as follows.

Stop the Foot up with Common Tar alone made warm; and repeat the same every fourth day, until the Foot is thoroughly grown to its former strength again. Then make use of the Healing Foot-mixture, see page 168, if occasion require the use of it.

For a FOOT that Proves FIGGY or SPUNGY after UNSOLING.

First dab the Foot with Oil of Turpentine; then take Common Tar one pint, and Common Allum three ounces, in fine powder, mixed together cold for use; when used, warm the above, then stop the Foot up with the above, and repeat the same every other day, in all respects as above directed; the above method will destroy the Fig, and cause the Foot to grow firm when the Wound begins to incarnate, and the pain is abated, make use of the Healing Foot-mixture, see page 168, as it is there recommended in all respects.

Section, 63.

Of HORSES FOUNDERED in the FEET, or, CORNS in the FEET, or a SHATTERED BRITTLE FOOT.

IN the firſt place dreſs and pare the Fore-feet quite thin with a Butteris; then with a drawing-knife, dreſs and pare the ſole-part, until the blood appears all over it; and if there ſhould be Corns, draw them well out, and waſh the ſole-part with Oil of Turpentine. Then take Venice Turpentine and Marſh Mallows Ointment, of each two ounces, mixed together cold for uſe; then ſpread the ſole-part of the Foot all over with the above Ointment, and lay a Bladder on the Foot; then ſet the ſhoe on the top of the Bladder, and ſtop the Foot up with dry Tow, upon the Bladder. Repeat the above dreſſing every other day, until the Foot is recovered to its former ſtrength again; keep the Horſe in a looſe ſtable, and do not ſtir him out for a fortnight at leaſt.

But if a ſevere pain from the effect of an injured Foot, and the Coronet ſeems to bulge out all around, make uſe as follows.

Take Oil of Origanum and the Strong Tincture of Euphorbium, of each one ounce mixed together; rub the Coronet-part all around with the above; and it will cauſe it to ſweat and ſcurf much; when the ſcurf comes clear off, repeat the ſame again.

To

Of HUMORS in the FORE-FEET.

To make a SHATTERED BRITTLE FOOT Grow STRONG and TOUGH.

Take Oil of Amber, and Oil of Petre, of each one ounce, and Goofe Oil five ounces, mixed together for ufe; then obferve to drefs and pare the Foot, until the blood appears all over the fole-part; then liquor the Foot well within and without with the above mixture; and heat it in with a hot iron, on the fole-part of the Foot; then lay a Bladder on the fole-part; and fet on the fhoe, and ftop the Foot up with dry Hurds upon the Bladder. Repeat the above dreffing in four days time, and keep the Horfe in for ten or twelve days at leaft; then give him gentle walking exercife, until his Foot is recovered to its former ftrength again. Wafh and dab all brittle fhattered Feet, with Old Sour Lant three times a-day, and make ufe of no Greafe but after a hard day's work, for Greafe is hurtful to a brittle Foot.

Section, 64.

Of HUMORS DROPPED into the FORE-FEET and LEGS by Hard TRAVELLING in Hot Dry SUMMERS, by Severity of Hard RACH-WORK.

HORSES are very fubject to Humors in their Fore-feet and Legs; efpecially when a Horfe is full in flefh, juft out of the dealer's Hands, or any other Horfe in the like condition; and if a Horfe of the above kind is rattled along on the road, efpecially when the ground is dry and hard, he will appear to the rider like a dog fhook in the fhoulders. Firft take

Of HUMORS in the FORE-FEET.

take the four shoes off, and tack them on again with four nails slack and easy. But should the Coronet-part appear to issue out a thin water resembling blood and seem to cleave around between the hair and the hoof from the effects of severe work, make use as follows.

Rub the Coronets of the Fore-feet, with Oil of Origanum one ounce, and Tincture of Euphorbium one ounce, mixed together for use; at the same time stop his Fore-feet up with Tar, Tallow and Horse Turpentine of each the same quantity made hot together, then make it into the consistence of a Stopping with Wheat Bran; then observe at the same time to bathe his Fore-legs and Pasterns with Spirits of Wine half a pint, Camphire two ounces, and sharp Vinegar three half pints, all mixed together for use; bathe the Sinews and Pasterns with the above mixture, then swaddle the Legs up with Flannel Rollers; and observe to bleed and give a few Pissing Balls, see page 27, and make use of a loose stable during the time of the cure.

The above applications will soon bring a Horse to rights in the above complaint. But if a Fever should appear from the violence of the pain, apply to the Section upon Fevers, see page 1, observing the directions there given, in every respect. But if the above case should prove obstinate, and the pain continue great, then the poor Creature is certain to shell his Fore-feet off, as so, he will be rendered useless for a whole twelve months, then it will be advisable to let him go to grass for the whole time without shoes on, then he may be useful again and not sooner.

Section,

Section, 65.

Of a CANKER in the FEET.

THE Canker in the Feet generally proceeds from a putrified Thrush that is got to a great head, infomuch that the Canker has eaten away the hufk or horny part of the Foot, halfway up to the Coronet and alfo at the fame time has fpread all over the fole-part.

First pare and drefs the Foot, and cut all the rotten part away with a Butteris and a drawing-knife; then wash the cankered part with the following sharp Water; then touch the rankeft part of the Canker with a feather dipped in Spirit of Common Salt, or Butter of Antimony; then ftop all the hollow crevices up tight with small pledgets of Tow dipped in the following Canker Ointment; and wedge them very tight into all the hollow parts and crevices; then tie a Cloth on with Fillets or ftrong Rollers to keep the dreffings on, as a Foot of this kind will not admit of a fhoe; repeat the above dreffings once a-day; and at the fame time bleed, and give a ftrong courfe of Piffing Balls, fee page 27, and repeat them according as they operate.

The SHARP WATER for the CANKER.

Take Verdigreafe, Roman Vitriol, and Roch Allum, of each one ounce, made into fine powder; boil the above in one quart of ftrong Verjuice; then for ufe.

The CANKER-OINTMENT.

Take Honey one pound, Verdigreafe two ounces, made into fine powder, Spirit of Common Salt one ounce, and Sublimate Mercury three drams, in fine powder, all mixed together in a mortar cold; then for ufe; and at the fame time touch the rankeft part of the Canker with Butter of Antimony, or Spirit of Common Salt fparingly with a feather, if occafion may require the ufe of it.

Section, 66.

Of GENERAL RULES Concerning GREASING and STOP-PING HORSES' FEET, and the Error of GREASING FEET too often.

GROOMS and other men in the care of Horfes, when they have a Horfe with tender Feet, they will hold it beft to greafe and ftop them up every night, which is a great error; for by fuch practice the Feet are brought as foft as a Puff-ball, and fo tender that they are not able to tread on the beft of exercife, much more unable to travel or hunt; nor is Greafe proper for the Feet at any time, except the night after a hard day's work, fuch as after a fweat or hunting, travelling, &c. or when the roads are very dry and hard; then greafe the Feet and ftop them up with their own Muck, when it drops warm from them; and at no other times to make ufe of Greafing and Stopping; except the Foot has met with a Wound or fome other injury; then it muft be treated as

fymptoms

Of GREASING and STOPPING FEET.

fymptoms require; or when a Horfe has to ftand a long time in the ftable, from an accident or lamenefs; then it would be proper to keep his Feet greafed and ftopped up with hot Stopping; a Horfe's Feet were never meant to be kept foft with Greafe and hot Stopping; but however I will endeavour to explain a better method which is as follows; and they, who will make a trial of the following method for two months, will perceive the Feet to grow tough and firm, and able for bufinefs. Obferve to keep in the ftable in readinefs, a two-gallon pot full of Old Lant; then wafh the Feet with the faid Lant within and without, three times a-day; and if the Feet are extraordinary bad, wafh and dab them with the Lant, fix or eight times in the fpace of one day; the above method is much fuperior to greafing of Feet, in every refpect; but when you make ufe of cold Stopping it may be as follows.

Take Horfe Muck whilft warm and old Lant, mix them together in a Stopping-box for ufe. When you mean to ufe cold Stopping, make ufe of the above, and no other fort whatever. But if there fhould be occafion for hot Stopping for a Foot when wounded, make ufe of the following.

Take Tar, Tallow, and Horfe Turpentine, of each the fame quantity made hot together, then make it into the confiftence of a Stopping with Wheat Bran; then for ufe; make ufe of the above as occafion may require.

The above Stopping is proper for a Wound or bruife in the Foot and to be made ufe of at no other times whatever.

APPENDIX.

APPENDIX.

SOME USEFUL AND WELL-PROVED
RECEIPTS,
FOR
COWS AND BEASTS.

For a HASKING CALF or COW.

TAKE Old Sour Lant one quart, and give it as a drink for nine mornings together for a Calf; and if for a Cow or Bullock give two quarts of Lant every morning fasting, for nine mornings together, first take blood.

For a COW or BEAST that makes BLOODY WATER.

Take Watergruel two quarts, Oil of Turpentine two ounces, Bole Armoniac two ounces and Electuary of Vitriol one meat-spoonful for one dose; to be repeated every other day, and three doses to be given.

For a COW that makes BLOODY WATER.

Take Skim-milk one quart, Common Salt one pint, the Juice of Nettles half a pint, and mix them all together cold for one drink; to be repeated every other day, give three drinks.

For a COW or BEAST that makes BLOODY or BLACK WATER.

Take a large handful of the Roots of White Briney; clean them and slice them, and pound them in a mortar; then boil them in two quarts of Sweet Milk, and give it as a drink; repeat the same for three mornings together.

For a SCOURING COW.

Take a double handful of the tender Twigs of Oak-bark, and boil it in two quarts of Water until it consumes to one quart; then add to the strained decoction, Diascordium two ounces, Roch Allum one ounce, and Bole Armoniac two ounces all in fine powder, and mix the whole together for one dose; give three doses, one every other day, and keep short of Water.

For a SCOURING COW.

Take Skim-milk half a pint, Verjuice half a pint, Roch Allum one ounce and a half and Bole Armoniac two ounces in fine powder, mix these all together cold for one dose; to be given every other day, give three doses

For a SCOURING COW.

Take a moderate sized sheet of strong brown packing Paper, dip it in Ale and pound it in a mortar all to pulp, then add a quart of Ale to the above, and warm the whole and give it as a drink; to be repeated for three days together.

For a COW that has LICKED UP some VENOMOUS ANIMAL, or is OVERGORGED with CLOVER-GRASS.

First bleed, then take Castile Soap two ounces, and Sirup of Marsh Mallows three ounces; let these be mixed together, and dissolved in a pint of warm Ale and given as a drink; then

then walk the Cow about very gently, and it will foon caufe her to empty herfelf plentifully.

To Caufe a COW to CLEANSE after CALVING.

Take Birthwort two ounces, Bay-berries two ounces, Myrrh one ounce, and Spermaceti two ounces; let the above be mixed together in fine powder and divided for two drinks; to be given in a quart of Ale, for two mornings together.

An OINTMENT for SORE DUGS.

Take Primrofe Leaves and Flowers, Foxglove Leaves and Flowers, Plantane, Allheal, and Chickweed, of each a full handful, pound the above Herbs together to a pulp, in a mortar, then add two or three pounds of Butter without Salt, then fimmer the above together over a flow fire for half an hour; then ftrained and preft for ufe; fmear the Dugs after milking night and morning. The above Ointment is cooling and healing.

For a Frefh GARGET in the UDDER.

Take a full pint of Common Salt and fry it in a frying-pan, to a Blacknefs, then pour the Salt into a quart of cold Water, and ftir it well, then give it to the Beaft. Repeat the above for three or four mornings together; firft bleed plentifully. The fymptoms of the above at firft, are a quaking and fhivering

For a Severe GARGET in a COW's UDDER.

Firft bleed plentifully, then make a Fomentation of the Grounds of Beer, and all the Emolient Herbs that can be got, and foment the Udder, and after each Fomentation rub the Udder with the following Ointment.

Take

Take Flanders Oil of Bays one pound, Goose Oil and Oil of Turpentine of each half a pint, Linseed Oil one pint, Spirits of Wine strongly camphorated four ounces, the Ointment of Elder and Mallows, and the Ointment of Populion of each six ounces, and Laurel-leaves a large double handful bruised; boil the whole together and strain it for use, stirring it until cold; if the above doth not answer a cure, cut a hole in one or all the four quarters of the Udder, then thrust into each hole a piece of Black Hellebore, and then a piece of Bacon dipped in Tar; these means will throw out a core, and with the help of the above Ointment will cause a cure.

For the FOULS in a COW's CLAW.

First cleanse the part well with a hair-rope, then dress the part with a feather dipped in Spirits of Common Salt, then lay to the part a pledget of dry Tow and tie it on with a cloth; keep the Beast in a dry house for two days.

For a COW FALLING after CALVING.

Take French Brandy one pint, and White Wine three half pints mixed together, rub her loins well with half a pint of the above mixture, then lay a Blanket in four doubles on her Loins and rub it with a panful of Hot Coals for half an hour, then give the remainder of the mixture as a drink adding to it, Long Pepper one ounce, and Grains of Paradise in powder one ounce, then cover her well with Blankets; the above will sweat her much, keep her close covered and give her nothing until such time she gets up of her own accord; then keep her warm and give her all comfortable things.

To STOP a COW from CASTING CALF.

Take Crude Antimony one ounce in fine powder, Bole Armoniac two ounces in powder, and Wood-ashes a full single handful;

handful; boil the above in one quart of Beef Brine, then add Oil of Turpentine one ounce and mix the whole together, and ftir it well with a fpoon. Then bleed the Cow, and while fhe is bleeding, bathe and rub her Loins with the above, and let it be rubbed on well with a man on each fide of her. The above is for one Cow, fo according to the number you mean to drefs you muft have the fame quantity for each.

For the YELLOWS on a COW.

Take Skim-milk one quart, and Strong Beer one pint; let them be boiled together and ftrained, then add to the Poffet, Caftile Soap one ounce and a half, Turmeric two ounces, and Saffron one dram, chopped fmall and mixed all together for one drink. Give three drinks, one every other morning, firft bleed the Cow.

A DRINK for a WEAKNESS and a WASTE.

Take Plantane, Knot-grafs, Wormwood, Salendine and Rue, of each a fmall handful, and boil them in two quarts of Ale, then ftrain and prefs the Herbs out well, and add Diapente one ounce, Grains of Paradife half an ounce, Annifeed and Carraway of each one ounce; to be given for one drink and repeated every other day.

For a COW that is MAW-BOUND or COSTIVE.

Take Caftile Soap, and Sirup of Marfh Mallows, of each two ounces mixed together in a mortar; diffolve the above in two quarts of Sweet Whey, and add Lenitive Electuary two ounces, Common Treacle one pound, Goofe Oil one pint, and Jalap in powder four drams; make the whole warm together and give it for one drink, and let it be worked off with Watergruel.

APPENDIX.

For a COW that is MAW-BOUND or COSTIVE.

Take Glauber's Salts three ounces, Lenitive Electuary three ounces, Cream of Tartar two ounces, Salt of Tartar three drams, Jalap four drams, Common Treacle one pound, Goofe Oil one pint. Give the above for one drink, in three pints of Sweet Whey, and work it off with Watergruel; to be given with a horn.

For the BLAIN.

Take Blood as foon as poffible, then immediately mix Common Salt two fingle handfuls, with Sour Lant two quarts, and give it as a drink; then rake the Beaft behind, and if there are any blood bladders in the Fundament-part up to the Loin-part, break them gently with your fingers' ends.

For the MOOR-EVIL.

The fymptoms of the above are a great ficknefs, and the Cow will make bloody Water and red Milk: take a red Herring or a fmall piece of dry hung Beef, and pound it in powder, then add Flour of Muftard three ounces, the fine Flour from a Tanner's Mill three ounces, Wood Charcoal in fine powder three ounces, and Britifh Oil fix pennyworth, let thefe be mixed all together and given in two quarts of warm Ale for one drink; one drink will perform the cure; obferve not to bleed in the above cafe.

For the BUSTION FOULS in a COW's CLAW.

Take White Lily Roots, Wormwood, and Plantane, of each a fmall handful, and bruife them in a mortar, then add as much rufty Bacon as will form the whole into a ftiff ball and apply it to the Claw with a Cloth tied round it. Repeat the

fame,

fame, once a-day until the part is burſt open, then dreſs it with Common Salt and Soft Soap, of each an equal quantity, mixed together, and tied to the part with a ſtrong Cloth. The above, being repeated will ſuck and heal it firm.

THE

CONCLUSION.

Having had Experience in Farriery, in the Services of the beſt of Maſters for ſeveral Years paſt, and even ſtill continue my Practice; I therefore thought proper by the Deſire of my Friends, to ſet the whole of this Work in as plain and eaſy a Manner to the Reader as poſſible, inſomuch that no Man that is a Groom can make the leaſt Miſtake.

I think it my Duty to my Friends and Gentlemen, and the whole World, to explain the Whole, in ſo perfect a Manner, as to be underſtood by all of thoſe Gentlemen who have any Idea in Farriery.

And in Time to come, when I am no more, there will without a Doubt be ſome pretending Perſons, who will reflect or rail againſt this Work without a Cauſe; but I do aſſure may Friends and Gentlemen,

CONCLUSION.

tlemen, that upon Trial of this Work, they will find every Section to answer in all Respects as I have stated the Case therein.

I could have swelled this Work much larger; but my chief Study was to insert all that lay in my Power, of what is most useful and necessary, throughout the whole Work.

And it may be well assured that I have used my best Endeavours to render the Whole as intelligible as possible, and flatter myself, the Reader will be so candid as to excuse any Error or Omission that may occur to him in the Perusal of this Work.

Honorable Gentlemen, I have no more to add, but that I hope to be esteemed,

Your sincere humble Servant and Wellwisher,

William Griffiths.

THE
INDEX.

Section.		Page
1. Of the Pulse of a Horse, and Fevers in General,		1
2. Of Staggers and Convulsions,		6
3. Of Yellows or Jaundice		10
4. Of Clysters of Various Sorts,		12
5. Of Purging Physic of Various Sorts,		15
6. Of Alterative Purges,		21
7. Of Alterative Balls,		23
8. Of Pissing Balls and Drinks,		26
9. Of Cordial Balls and Cordial Drinks of Various Sorts,		28
10. Of Balls and Drinks to relieve Old Coughs and Phthisics,		32
11. Of a Rattling and Stoppage in the Head,		35
12. Of Drinks to promote Perspiration,		37
13. Of Drinks for Sudden Accidents,		38
14. Of Body Strains,		39
15. Of a Lax or Scouring,		40
16. Of the Colic or Gripes,		43
17. Of the Pleurisy and Inflammation of the Lungs,		47
18. Of Hurts in the Kidneys, and Gravel in the Parts therefore,		49
19. Of a Diabetes or overflowing of the Urine,		51
20. Of the Strangles and Distemper.		52
21. Of Bots and Worms,		56
22. Of Broken-winded Horses,		60
23. Of Surfeits in General,		66
24. Of Farcies in General,		68
25. Of a Horse or Cow that has Licked up some Venomous Animal,		74
26. Of Glandered Horses,		75
27. Of a Horse burnt by a Mare,		78
28. Of the Anticor,		80
29. Of Wounds in General,		81
30. Of Ulcers in General or Swelling Tumors,		88
31. Of Inflammations and Mortifications,		92

32. Of

INDEX.

32. Of Wrenches or Strains in the Back or Loins, — — 95
33. Of the Scab or Mange, — — — — 96
34. Of Lice and Vermine, — — — — 98
35. Of Fresh Crushes from the Saddle, — — — 99
36. Of Diseases of the Eyes, — — — — 100
37. Of the Vives, — — — — 103
38. Of Bad Necks and Veins after Bleeding, — — 105
39. Of a Canker in the Mouth and Tail, — — — 107
40. Of Blisters of Various Sorts, — — — 108
41. Of Charges, — — — — — 112
42. Of the Poll-evil and Fistula, — — — 113
43. Of Lampas and Wolves Teeth and Flaps in the Mouth, — 118
44. Of Ornaments in General, — — — 119
45. Of Lameness, Strains or Bruises in the Shoulder, Whirlbone, &c. 124
46. Of Bowel-galls, — — — — — 133
47. Of Mallenders and Sellanders, — — — 134
48. Of Splents and Curbs, — — — — 136
49. Of Bone-spavins or Ringbones, — — — 139
50. Of Blood or Bog-spavins, — — — — 142
51. Of Strains in the Back Sinews, — — — 144
52. Of Strains in the Pastern or Coffin-joint, — — 148
53. Of Fractures or Broken Bones, — — — 150
54. Of Grapy Heels. — — — — — 151
55. Of the Grease, — — — — — 152
56. Of Heel-ointment, — — — — 154
57. Of a Cancerous Humor on the Legs and Heels, — 156
58. Of Quitter-bones, — — — — 157
59. Of Over-reaches or Fresh Stabs on the Coronet-part of the Foot, 161
60. Of Sand-cracks, — — — — 162
61. Of Running Thrushes in the Frog of the Foot, — 165
62. Of Wounds in General in the Feet, — — 166
63. Of Horses Foundered in the Feet, or Corns in the Feet, &c. 171
64. Of Humors dropped into the Fore-feet and Legs, &c. — 172
65. Of a Canker in the Feet, — — — — 174
66. Of general Rules concerning Greasing and Stopping Horse's Feet, 175
An Appendix of Receipts for Cows and Beasts, — — 177

AN ALPHABETICAL LIST,

OF THE

RECEIPTS.

	Page.
A.	
ALTERATIVE Purges,	21, 22
Alterative Balls,	23, 24
Alterative Mercurial Ball,	25
Alterative for a Lameness,	25
Anodyne Balsam,	32
Anticor,	· 80
B.	
Body Strains,	39, 40
Bots and Worms,	56, ·57, 58, 59
Broken-winded,	60, 61, 62, 63, 64, 65
Burnt by a Mare,	78, 79
Bleeding at the Nose and Stomach, to stop,	81
Blood in any Part, to stop,	82
Blood from a Wound, to stop,	82
Basilicon Yellow,	83
Balsam Friars, to make	84
Bone to Exfoliate,	85, 91
Back or Loins, Strains in,	95
Back, crushed by a Saddle,	99, 100
Bleeding, Bad Necks after,	105, 106
Blisters of various Sorts,	108
———— Mild,	108
———— Vitriol,	109
———— Strong for a Let-down Sinew,	109
———— after Firing,	109
———— Shoulder Strain,	110
———— Strong Liquid,	110
———— for a Bone Spavin,	110
Brine Embrocation for Strains,	127

Bang

An ALPHABETICAL LIST, &c.

Bang on any Part,	129, 131
Butterton's Water, to make,	129
Black Oils for old Strains,	130
Bowel Galls,	133, 134
Bone Spavin or Ringbones,	139
Blood or Bog Spavin,	142
Bog Spavin,	142
Bones Broken,	150
Brittle Feet,	171
Bloody Water, for a Cow that makes,	177, 178
Blain, for a Cow that has,	182

C.

Clyſters, of various Sorts,	12
——— Comfortable,	13
——— in a Fever,	13
——— for a Foal,	13
——— the Colic,	13
——— if Coſtive,	14
——— for an Inflammation in the Bowels,	14
——— Aſtringent,	14
Colds,	28
Cordial Balls and Drinks,	28
——— Braken's Ball,	28
——— for freſh taken Colds,	28
——— Drink for a Cold,	29
——— Drink for a tired Horſe	29, 30
——— Drink, a ſcouring thriving	30
——— Balls for Aguiſh Diſorders,	30
——— Drink for a loſt Appetite,	31
——— Drink, Aromatic Herbs,	31
——— Drink, to cauſe an Appetite,	31
Coughs and Phthiſics,	32, 33, 34
Colic or Gripes,	43, 44, 45, 46, 47
Core, to throw out,	91
Cauſtic Paper,	91
Cruſhes, by Saddle,	99, 100
Canker in the Mouth and Tail,	107
Charges,	112, 113
Cropping Ears,	120
Curbs and Splents,	136, 137, 138
Coffin-joint, ſtrained,	148, 149
Cancerous Humor on the Legs or Heels,	156
Coffin Bone, wounded,	168
	Corns

An ALPHABETICAL LIST, &c.

Corns in the Feet,	171
Canker in the Feet,	174
Cleanse after Calving, to cause,	179
Casting Calf, to stop a Cow,	180
Costive, a Cow that is,	181, 182

D.

Drink, Tar Water,	36
Diabetes, or Overflowing of the Urine.	51
Distemper and Strangles,	52, 53, 54, 55
Digestive Green Ointment,	82
Drying Powder,	85

E.

Exfoliate a Bone,	85, 91
Egyptiacum, to make,	90
Eyes, Diseases in,	100
—— Inflamed Humor in,	101
—— Water for,	101
—— Wounds in,	101
—— Vegeto Mineral Water for,	102
—— Film or Speck on,	102
—— Bruised,	103
Ears, to set,	120
Ears, to crop,	120
Elbow, the Symptoms of Lameness in,	125
Embrocations for Strains,	126, 127
Excrescences, hard,	138

F.

Fevers in General,	1
—— a Mild Clyster in,	2
—— a Drink for,	2
—— an Intermitting Compound,	3
—— Genuine Ball for,	3
—— Intermitting,	3
—— in the Recovery of,	4
—— to promote Urine in,	4
—— if Costive in,	4
—— in the Recovery,	4
—— Food, proper to be given,	5
—— Clyster in,	13
—— Malignant and Pestilent,	37
Fungous or Proud Flesh to destroy,	54, 84, 86, 91
Farcies in General,	68, 69, 70, 71, 72, 73
Fomentation for Wounds,	83, 90

Y y   Fomentation

An ALPHABETICAL LIST, &c.

Fomentation to disperse a Swelling,	84
Friars Balsam, to make,	84
Firing Blister, after,	109
Fistula and Poll-evil,	113
Flaps,	118, 119
Firing,	123
Foot, the Symptoms of Lameness in,	124
Fractures or Broken Bones,	150
Feet, Wounds in,	166, 167, 168, 169, 170
Foundered in the Feet,	171
Feet, Brittle,	171
Feet, Humors in,	172
Feet, Canker in,	174, 175
Fouls in a Cow's Claw,	180, 182
Falling after Calving,	180

G.

Gripes or Colic,	43, 44, 45, 46, 47
Gravel in the Kidneys,	49
Glandered Horses,	75, 76, 77
Galled Shoulders,	86
Gelding,	122
Gall Embrocation for Strains,	127
Grapy Heels,	151
Grease,	152, 153, 154
Greasing and Stopping Feet,	176
Garget in a Cow's Udder,	179

H.

Hiera Picra Spices Purge,	18
Head, rattling in,	35
Horse Burnt by a Mare,	78, 79
Hair, to cause to grow on fresh healed Wounds,	87
Hough, the Symptoms of Lameness in,	125
Hip, the Symptoms of Lameness in,	126
Hard Excrescences,	138
Hough, Sinus on,	143
Heels, Grapy,	151
Heel Ointments,	154, 155, 156
Heels, Cancerous Humors in,	156
Heels burnt in the Lime,	156
Humors in the Legs and Feet,	172
Hasking Cow or Calf,	177

I.

Jaundice or Yellows, the Cause and Symptoms of,	10

Jaundice

An ALPHABETICAL LIST, &c.

Jaundice, Drink for,	11
———— Balls for,	11
———— Drink for,	11
———— Balls for when Obstinate,	11
———— Balls for,	12
Inflamed Bowels, Clyster for,	14
Inflamed Bowels, Purge for,	19
Inflammation of the Lungs,	47
Jaw-Pifs,	51, 52
Joint Water, to Stop,	86
Inflammations and Mortifications,	92
Inflammation, a Fomentation for,	93
———— Embrocation for,	94
———— Vegeto Mineral Water,	94

K.

Kidneys, Hurts in,	49, 50
———— Gravel in,	49
Knee, Broken or Cut,	87, 90
Knee, Broken to cause Hair to grow on,	87
Knee, the Symptoms of Lameness in,	125

L.

Lax or Scouring,	40, 41, 42, 43
Lungs, Inflammation in,	47, 48
———— Pleurisy in,	47, 48
Loins or Back, Strains in,	95
Lice and Vermine,	98, 99
Lampas,	118, 119
Lameness, Symptoms of in all Parts,	124
Legs, Cancerous Humor in,	156
Legs, Humors in,	172

M.

Molten Greafe, a Purge for,	19
Matthew's Pill,	35
Mare, to take off her Pride,	79
Mare, to make her stand to Horse,	79
Myrrh Tincture of, to make,	85
Mortifications and Inflammations,	92
Mortification to stop,	94
Mange or Scab,	96, 97
Mouth, Canker in,	107
Mallenders and Sellanders,	134, 135
Maw-bound, a Cow that is,	181, 182
Moor-evil, for a Cow that has,	182

An ALPHABETICAL LIST, &c.

N.
Necks, bad after Bleeding, — — 105, 106
Nicking Tail, — — 122

O.
Overgorged with Clover, &c. — — 74, 178
Ointment, Green Digestive, — — 82
Ointment, a Healing Cleansing, — — 83
Ointment, Red Digestive, — — 89
Ointment, Strong Red Digestive, — — 89
Ornaments in General, — — 119
Opodeldoc, to make, — — 132
Ointments for the Heels, — 154, 155, 156
Over-reaches, — — 161, 162
Ointment for Cows fore Dugs, — — 179

P.
Pulse, — — 1
Physic of various Sorts, — — 15
—— Gentle Mild Purge, — — 15
—— Gentle Mild Purge, — — 16
—— Ditto, Ditto, — — 17
—— Strong safe Purge, — — 17
—— at Grafs, — — 18
—— the Hiera Picra Spices, — — 18
—— after a Sweat, — — 18
—— for the Molten Greafe, — — 19
—— for an Inflamed Bowel, — — 19
—— Mercurial Method of giving, — — 20
—— for a Lax or Scouring, — — 20
Pissing Balls and Drinks, — — 26, 27
Perspiration, Drink to promote, — — 37
Pleurify and Inflammation of the Lungs, — 47
Proud Flesh, to destroy, — 54, 84, 86, 91
Pride, to take a Mare off, — — 79
Poll-evil, — 113, 114, 115, 116, 117
Pain after Lameness, — — 132
Paftern ftrained, — — 148

Q.
Quitter Bones, — 157, 158, 159, 160

R.
Rattling in the Head, — — 35
Running at the Nofe, — — 35
Ringbones, — — 139, 140
Running Thrufhes, — — 165, 166

Staggers,

An ALPHABETICAL LIST, &c.

Staggers, the Cause and Symptoms of,	6
———— Draught for,	6
———— Clyster for,	7
———— Cooling Purge for,	7
———— Easy Purge for,	7
———— Ball for,	8
———— Paste for,	8
———— Proper food to be given,	9
———— For a wild Fit,	9
———— Clyster for,	12
Sweat, a Purge after,	18
Scouring, a Purge Astringent for,	20
Sweat, a Drink to promote,	37
Staggers, Tincture for,	37
Sudden Accidents, Drink for,	38
Strains, Body,	39
Scouring or Lax,	40, 41, 42, 43
Strangles and Distemper,	52, 53, 54, 55
Surfeits in general,	66, 67, 68
Swelling, a Fomentation to disperse,	84
Shoulders, Galled,	86
Swelling Tumors in general,	88
———— Poultice to ripen,	88, 89
Strains in the Back or Loins,	95
Saddle Crushes,	99, 100
Sinew Let-down, Blister for,	109
Shoulder Strain, Blister for,	110
Spavin, Blister for,	110, 111
Star, to make,	121
Setting a Tail,	122
Shoulder, the Symptoms of Lameness in,	125
Stifle, the Symptoms of Lameness in,	125
Strains fresh, Embrocation for,	126
Shoulder Strained,	128
Stifle Strained,	128
Strains, Old,	130, 131
Soap Embrocation,	132
Splents and Curbs,	136, 137, 138, 139
Spavins,	139, 140, 141
Sinews, Strained,	144, 145, 146, 147
Sand-cracks,	162, 163, 164
Stopping, Hot,	168
Stopping and Greasing Feet,	175, 176

Scouring

An ALPHABETICAL LIST, &c.

Scouring Cow, — 178
Sore Dugs, Ointment for, — 179

T.

Tar-Water Drink, — 36
Thick Winded Horses, Purge for, — 62
Tincture of Myrrh, to make, — 85
Tumour and Swellings in general, — 88
Tail, Canker in, — 107
Tail, to Set, — 122

U.

Urine, overflowing of, — 51, 52
Ulcer, Healing and Drying Powder for, — 85
Ulcers in general, — 88
———- Poultice to Ripen, — 88, 89
———- Foul, to Cleanse, — 91
Unsoling, method of, — 169
Udder, Garget in, — 179

V.

Venomous Animal Licked, — 74, 178
Vegeto Mineral Water, — 94
Vermine and Lice, — 98, 99
Vives, — 103, 104

W.

Wheesing in the Stomach, — 36
————— Nose Drink for, — 36
Worms and Bots, — 56, 57, 58, 59
Wind Broken or Thick, — 60, 61, 62, 63, 64, 65
Wounds in general, — 81, 82, 83, 84, 85, 86, 87
————- Fomentation for, — 83
————- Healing and Drying Powder for, — 85
Wolves Teeth, — 118, 119
Whirlbone, the Symptoms of Lameness in, — 126
Wounds in the Feet, — 166
Weakness, a Drink for a Cow, — 181

Y.

Yellows or Jaundice, — 10
Yellows in a Cow, — 181

A LIST

OF THE

SUBSCRIBERS.

Sir Watkin Williams Wynn, Bart. Wynnstay.
Earl Grosvenor, Eaton-hall.
Lord Belgrave, Ditto.
Sir Robert Vaughan, 2 Copies.
Sir Thomas Hanmer, Bettisfield.
Lord Warwick, Warwickshire.
Lord Bagot, Blighfield.

A.

Mr. Ellis Allington, Berfe.
Mr. Adams, Paper-maker, Hanmer.

B.

Ambrofe Brooks, Efq. Edge.
Henry Ellis Botes, Efq. Pen ŷ lan.
—— Burgany, Efq.
Mr. Bowen, Ofweftry.
Mr. Price Bythell.
Mr. Bowen, Sontley.
Mr. Benion, Chalton.
Mr. James Boydell, Trevallyn.
Mr. William Boydell, Ditto.
Mr. Jofeph Boydell, Roffet Green.
Mr. Boot, Monfley.
Mr. William Bradfhaw, Newton.
Mr. John Bafter, Sealand.
Mr. Thomas Birch, Grocer, Ellefmere.
Mr. Beale Blackwell, King-ftreet, Clerkenwell, London.
Mr. Barker, Erbiftock-hall.
Mr. Barker, Kiddington Green.
Mr. Thomas Birchall, Groom to Salifbury Vaughan, Efq.
Mr. Thomas Billinge, Pemberton, near Wigan, Lancafhire.
Mr. Benion, Old Sontley.

C.

Thomas Cuming, Efq. Brynŷpys.
Thomas Cafe, Efq. 2 Copies.
—— Clark, Efq. Cholmondley.

SUBSCRIBERS.

Mr. John Croxton, Ofweftry.
Mr. Richard Croxton, Ditto.
Mr. Clay, Farrier, Wem.
Mr. Thomas Crewe, Marchwiel.
Mr. Henry Cheney, Penbedw.
Mr. Charles Cheatham, Marchwiel.
Colonel Cholmondley, Vale Royal.

D.
William Davenport, Efq. Chefter.
Rev. Mr. Dixon, Felton.
Rev. Mr. W. Davies, Whittington.
Mr. Daniel Dean, Groom at Afton.
Mr. Thomas Dale, Saddler, Ofweftry.
Mr. Thomas Darricote, Chefter.
Mr. Thomas Davies, Trewilan.

E.
John Evans, Efq. Gardden, near Ruabon.
Mr. Samuel Evans, Bryn ŷr owen.
Mr. Edwards, Stanfty.

F.
Phillip Fletcher, Efq. Gwernhailed.
Mr. Richard Francis, Vicarage, Ruabon.
Mr. Thomas Fallows, Booth-hall, near Cheadley.
Mr. Samuel Edwards, Groom, to Edward Faulkner, Efq. Fairfield, Lancafhire.
Mr. Edward Francis, Ofler at the Eagles, Wrexham,

G.
John Griffith, Efq. Holt-ftreet, Wrexham.

Mr. Edward Griffiths, Coachman, Ofweftry.
Mr. Willam Grice, Newton, Chefhire, 2 Copies.
Mr. Thomas Griffiths, Penley.

H.
———— Humberfton, Efq. Gwerfyllt.
Owen Hornfby, Efq. Porkington.
John Humphreys, Efq. Llwyn.
Mr. Richard Hanfon, Pláfpower.
Mr. Nathaniel Harris, Halkin.
Mr. Thomas Hughes, Pláfnewydd.
Mr. Humphrey Hughes, Allthray.
Mr. Roger Hughes, Porkington.
Mr. Corbet Harris, Corwen.
Mr. Roger Hughes, Allthray.
Mr. Edward Harries, Shrewfbury.
Mr. John Hows, Chudleigh, Devonfhire.

I.
John Jones, Efq. Pen-ŷ-bryn.
Richard Jones, Efq. Bellon Place.
Lewis Jones, Efq. Attorney, Ofweftry.
Randle Jones, Efq. New-hall.
Mr. William Jackfon, Farrier, Hanmer.
Mr. Jones, Lightwood-hall.
Mr. W. Jones, Ironmafter, Gardden.
Mr. John ————, Groom at Halfton.
Mr. John Jackfon, Roden's Hall, Is ŷ Coed.
Mr. David Jones, Llanfyllin.
Mr. Edward Jones, Borras-hall.
Mr. Thomas Jones, Flaxdreffer, Wrexham.

SUBSCRIBERS.

Mr. John Jeffreys, at Mrs. Lloyd's, Mold.
Mr. Thomas Jackſon, Wynnſtay.
Mr. Jackſon, Plâſpower.
Mr. Nathaniel Jones, Havodùnos.
Mr. Hampton Jones.
Mr. Jones, Coed ŷ Glŷn

K.
John Kynaſton, Eſq. Hardwick.
Mr. Trim Kent, Sandford.

L.
John Lloyd, Eſq. Havodùnos.
Peter Lloyd, Eſq. Is ŷ Coed.
John Leeche, Eſq. Stretton.
William Leeche, Eſq. Carden.
Robert Lloyd, Eſq. Swanhill.
Trevor Lloyd, Eſq. Trevor-hall.
William Lloyd, Eſq. Plâſpower.
Edward Lloyd, Eſq. Pen-ŷ-lan.
Rev. John Robert Lloyd, Aſton.
Mrs. Lloyd, Havodùnos.
Miſs Lloyd, Ditto.
Mr. John Lloyd, Hoole.
Mr. John Leigh, Steward, Hardwick.
Mr. John Lloyd, Accrevair.
Mr. John Lloyd, Holywell.
Mr. Thomas Lovett, Chirk.
Mr. Leiceſter.

M.
Richard Myddelton, Eſq. Chirk Caſtle.
John Mytton, Eſq. Halſton.
Mr. William Mytton, Rochdale, Lancaſhire.

T. Trevor Mathers, Trevor-hall.
Mr. John Marſden, Groom to the Duke of Bedford.
Mr. John Manlove, Ternhill.
Mr. Edward Meaſon.
Mr. John Manlove, Hampton.
Mr. George Miller, Groom to Richard Myddelton, Eſq.
Mr. Samuel Morgan, Coachman, to Mrs. Puleſton, Wrexham.
Mr. William Morris, Plas ŷn ŷ Pentre.

N.
Mr. Nickſon, the Stocks,
Mr. Robert Nickſon, Halghton.
Mr. Richard Nickſon, Agdon.
Mr. Robert Newell, Cheſter.

P.
Richard Puleſton, Eſq. Emral.
——— Pennant, Eſq. Roſchill.
Rev. Mr. Price, Chirk.
Rev. Mr. Potter, Soughton.
Rev. Mr. Parks, Hanmer.
Dr. Phillips, Malpas.
Mr. Thomas Poole, Eyton.
Mr. John Pertham, Groom at Emral.
The Coachman, at Ditto,
Mr. Poyſer, Worthenbury.
— John Price, Newton.
— Davies, Farrier and Blackſmith, Elleſmere.
— Samuel Price, Horſley.
— Ellis Parry, Is ŷ Coed.
— John Pearſon, Ditto.
— John Page, Barkhampſtead.
— Joſeph Payton, Hawkſton.

SUBSCRIBERS.

Mrs. Jane Parks, Llangollen.

R.
Owen Roberts, Esq. Wem.
Counsellor Richards, London,
Mr. Edward Rees, Oswestry.
— Watkin Rees, Rhos Llany-chrygog.
— Wm. Roberts, Caroline Wharf, Rotherhithe, Surry.
— Thomas Rowland, Corwen.
— Sam. Read, Conway, 2 Copies.
— Thomas Roberts, Borras-head.
— Wm. Roberts, Gerwin vechan.
— Wm. Roberts, Groom at Swan-hill.
— John Rowland, Havod y Bwch.
— Dan. Rowland, Carden Green.
— Thomas Rowley, at Ld. Pawlett's.
— John Roberts, Newhall.
— Roberts, Gerwin.
— Roberts, of the Five Fords.
— Richardson, Beeston.

S.
Mr. William Smith, Groom at Mr. Botes's.
— Joseph Stubbs, Vale Royal.
— William Smele, Coachman, at Earl Carisford's, London.
— Samuel Sidebotham, Farndon.
— Edward Spencer, Chester.
— James Smith, Allthray.
— Rowe Smith, Allington.
— Watkin Samuel, Plàs gôch.

T.
Rev. Thomas Trevor, Whittington.
Mr. James Tate, Barkhampstead.
— William Turner, Whitchurch.
— John Thomas, Eccleston.
— John Thomas, Attorney, Llan-fyllin.
— Thomas, Steward at Hartsheath.
— Charles Tomkins, Gwersyllt.

V.
Salisbury Vaughan, Esq.
Griffith Vaughan, Esq.
Mr. John Valentine, Wrexham.

W.
Charles Watkin Williams Wynn, Esq.
John Wynn, Esq. Ryton.
John Williams, Esq. Havod y Bwch.
―――― Wardle, Esq. Hartsheath.
Rev. Morris Wynn, Wenlock.
Captain Williams, Hardwick.
Dr. Wilkinson, Wrexham.
Mr. Thomas Weavor, Manchester.
— Richard Whitfield, Comer.
— Wynn, Cricket.
— Williams, Rhŷd y Cilgwin.
— Charles Woollam, Wrexham.
— Charles Wild, Bettisfield.

Y.
Phillip Yorke, Esq. Erthig.
Simon Yorke, Esq. Ditto.

Z.
Mr. Charles Zachary, Burton.

www.ingramcontent.com/pod-product-compliance
Lightning Source LLC
Chambersburg PA
CBHW020906230426
43666CB00008B/1337